KT-474-027

A Practical Guide to Activities for Young Children

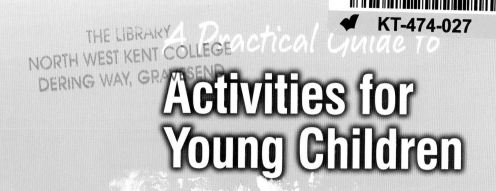

...tion

Christine Hobart

Jill Frankel

Series Editor: Miranda Walker

Nelson Thornes

First published in 1995 by:
Stanley Thornes (Publishers) Ltd
Second edition 1999
Third edition published 2005 by Nelson Thornes Ltd

This edition published 2009 by:
Nelson Thornes Ltd
27 Bath Road
Cheltenham
GL53 7TH
United Kingdom

12 13 / 10 9 8 7 6 5 4 3 2

A catalogue record for this book is available from the British Library.

ISBN 978 1 4085 0486 4

Cover photograph by Jim Wileman
Photography by Martin Sookias
Page make-up by Florence Production Ltd, Stoodleigh, Devon
Printed in China

Contents

Introduction

This is not a theoretical book about play and learning experiences, although each chapter has a short general introduction. It is a highly practical guide to all activities that should be available to young children from 0 to 7:11 years and is laid out in an accessible format.

Since 2008 *The Early Years Foundation Stage* (EYFS) has been mandatory for all schools and all early years providers in Ofsted registered settings. It applies to children from birth to the end of the academic year in which the child has their fifth birthday. This new edition has been fully revised and features an overview of the EYFS. Links to the EYFS are also made within the activities.

Part 1, which describes how you work professionally, should help you to evaluate your practice and to ensure that you are always aware of anti-discriminatory practice and new educational initiatives.

Part 2, which covers activities for babies and toddlers, has been extended to link in with the EYFS. It is important that childcare and education practitioners have a sound understanding of the emotional needs of babies, and provide appropriate enriching and stimulating activities.

Part 3 examines activities for young children that promote and extend all areas of their development, following the EYFS Curriculum.

Part 4 looks at the school-aged child both in school following the National Curriculum and in out-of-school settings.

The book concludes with a brief look at course work.

Tables are included to show at a glance the amount and type of space required for each experience and the type of play the activity should promote. Supervision by an adult is necessary for all play experiences, but some will gain more from closer adult involvement and interest than others.

The book includes lists showing what materials are essential and suggests additional equipment. Always buy the best quality equipment that can be afforded. When using items reflecting other cultures, you must be aware of any cultural or religious significance attached to them, and use them in an appropriate way.

The value of each activity to the child is outlined, ensuring that a broad curriculum will be offered and that all areas of development and learning are encouraged and promoted. This is especially useful if you have a child who appears to be delayed in one area of development, as you will be able to see very quickly how to help. Another child may be gifted in one or more areas of development and learning, and may need additional stimulation and opportunities for extended exploration.

There is an emphasis on good practice and the role of the adult, highlighting factors that are important in your planning, presentation and evaluation of the experiences you offer children. When working with children, life is not always predictable, and from time to time plans may go awry. Do not be despondent, learn from your mistakes and try again.

All activities, equipment, toys, games and books must reflect our diverse society, and you need to be aware of children who may have particular special needs. Whatever you are presenting should be seen as part of the everyday environment, and not as something exotic and different. The sections on anti-discrimination will help you to focus on these matters.

The environment in which you work needs to be a safe and pleasant place. The paragraphs pointing out safety factors should help you to be aware of any potential hazards, either in the room or in the equipment chosen.

At the end of each chapter, a 'Partnership with parents' section highlights areas where you might work together with parents.

At the end of each chapter a useful resource list of books and websites has been added, and there is a larger general resource list. A glossary of terms emboldened in the text will be found at the end of the book.

Acknowledgements

The authors would like to thank Teresa O'Dea, Cynthia Isaac and Anna Mennell for their time and generosity.

We are particularly grateful to students at Oaklands College, Elizabeth Gormley for the curriculum and detailed activity plans (pages 165–9) and to Sarah Clarke for the routine (pages 169–75).

We also thank Wendy Ewer for the Checklist for Books and Stories on pages 101–2 and Julie Howarth for reading and commenting on the infant school section.

Many thanks to the staff and children at Treetops Nursery, Cheltenham, for their fun and enthusiasm during the photoshoot.

Thanks also to Naunton Park Primary School, particularly Giles Clare, Mrs Bradshaw and the Blue Class.

The publishers are indebted to the following for permission to reproduce photographs:

Page 26: Adult reading to a small baby (A1H910 – RF) copyright © BananaStock/Alamy.

Page 28: Treasure basket. Thanks to the Cotter family and especially to Noah Cotter.

Page 36: Girl sweeping while parents watch (RF241991) copyright © Royalty-Free/CORBIS

Page 54: Teacher helps Japanese American six-year old girl hammer a nail (A4B9C9 – L) copyright © David Young-Wolff/Alamy.

Page 110: Three children in exercise/dance class (PE-037-0111) copyright © Ariel Skelley/CORBIS

Page 124: A mother walks her two children in a park (ACX680 – L) copyright © Adrian Sherratt/Alamy

Page 135: Hindu children – Southall – eating sweets (10550064) copyright © Art Directors/TRIP

Page 150: Group of children working together on a project (A92671 – L) copyright © Janine Wiedel Photolibrary/Alamy

About the Authors

Christine Hobart and Jill Frankel come from a background of health visiting and nursery education. They worked together in Camden before meeting again at City and Islington College. They have worked together for many years, training students to work with young children and have written 12 books encompassing all areas of the childcare curriculum. Christine is an external examiner for CACHE.

Miranda Walker has worked with children from birth to 16 years in a range of settings, including her own day nursery and out of school clubs. She has inspected nursery provision for OFSTED, and worked at East Devon College as an Early Years and Playwork lecturer and NVQ assessor and internal verifier. She is a regular contributor to industry magazines and an established author.

Part 1

Working Professionally

When you provide activities for children, whether this provision is in the family setting as a nanny, childminder or home carer, or in pre-schools, nurseries and schools, it is important to understand why you are doing so, and appreciate the benefits to children's **development** and learning. A professional childcare and education worker will be aware of the latest educational initiatives, current and past research, and the importance of providing activities within the framework of a **curriculum**.

Working in a professional manner involves careful planning and preparation of all activities, thoughtful and flexible **implementation**, and a thorough **evaluation** of each activity that in turn contributes to future planning.

1 The Professional Framework

Much of the work that is carried out with young children in your establishment is in the form of activities, most of which are provided and structured by the staff team. Some can be unstructured and spontaneous and allow the children to use their imagination and develop close **peer** relationships.

The value of activities for young children

The activities that you provide should promote the children's all-round development and learning, and be both well planned and well prepared. You will need to take time to evaluate the outcomes of the activities, which should be **age-appropriate** and reflect our diverse society. All the children should have equal access to all of the activities, regardless of language fluency, racial origin, gender, culture, class or disability.

Consultation and planning is necessary with other members of the team, so that **milestones** are recognised, Early Learning Goals are achieved and the requirements of the National Curriculum are fulfilled. Your observations of children, both individually and in a group, will also play a major part in determining the particular activity you might plan to do.

Planning your activities includes making sure that:

- you have sufficient materials for the whole class or group to take part, if they should so wish
- there is time to carry out the activity to a satisfactory conclusion
- there is sufficient suitable space available
- there is another adult free to help you, if the activity requires it.

Using this book should help you to plan and prepare activities efficiently, and to be aware of the development and learning outcomes for the children for each of the activities you choose to do. **Anti-discriminatory practice**, the individual needs of children and safety must always be in the forefront of your mind in any work you plan with the children.

When you have completed an activity, you need to take time to think carefully and **objectively** about how the children responded, what they learnt, and what areas of development were promoted and extended. Even a disaster can be a positive learning experience for you and will improve the quality of your future practice.

Make sure you participate in offering the full range of activities. Practice makes perfect! For example, if you avoid music sessions as a student, it will be more difficult for you to provide them once you are qualified.

The value of play

We all like to play. As an adult, you probably play games, exercise, dance, paint, sew or knit, go on holiday, visit museums and art galleries, and take part in passive activities, such as watching television, going to the cinema and theatre, listening to music and reading. Most people find these activities stimulating and that they add to their enjoyment of life. Children need the same opportunities, as it is mainly by play that children learn.

Children's play has been called 'children's work' and it shows adults what children can understand and do. Play is an essential part of children's daily life and promotes all-round development. Through play, the child experiences life and learns to understand the world and her place in it. Play can be social, when children play with each other.

The baby plays from birth, the first 'toy' being the mother's breast. Play develops through several stages:

- solitary (on her own)
- parallel (playing alongside another child or adult)
- associative play (playing with other children)
- cooperative play, playing with others and involving planning and games with complicated rules.

Be creative and imaginative

Play alongside or cooperatively with other children

Communicate

Investigate and discover

Understand the need for rules

Be happy

Learn self-control

Express fears or actual experiences in a safe environment

PLAY ALLOWS CHILDREN TO . . .

Care for others

Develop and express new ideas

Take risks

Explore

Practise and develop skills

Develop concentration

Express negative feelings

Make sense of the world

Learn

Share

There are many different types of play. These include:

- structured play, where the adult chooses the activity, provides the materials and organises the play
- spontaneous play, when the child chooses to play on the spur of the moment
- child-centred play, where the child chooses the activity
- heuristic play, where toddlers explore various objects without adult intervention
- imitative play, the beginning of imaginary play, where a baby copies what she has seen an adult doing, such as waving 'Bye bye'
- domestic play, often in the role play corner, such as pretending to make cups of tea and sweeping the floor. This is usually carried out by the pre-school age group, and can be solitary, or with other children or adults
- messy play, which often involves exploring materials with the hands or other parts of the body
- play with natural materials, such as sand, water, wood, clay and mud
- imaginative play, which involves creative thought
- repetitive play, where the child feels the need to repeat an activity over and over again, until she feels satisfied

- creative play, including art work and model making
- energetic physical play, usually taking place outside
- organised games, which include ring games and board games, and often have rules.

For children, passive play such as watching DVDs is not as valuable as active play in which they take part. This is not to say that there is no place for television, but screen time should certainly be restricted, particularly for young children, who should preferably watch with an adult who helps her to understand what is happening and answer her questions. All programmes should be suitable for the child's age and stage and development. Most daycare settings for children under the age of five choose not to have a television.

The role of the adult

Adults supervising children's play and practical activities have an important and sensitive role to play. They need to be aware of the value of all activities to the children's development and learning, and plan and prepare them thoroughly. Students need to understand the difference between adult interaction and intervention. The adult who plays and interacts with the child will usually extend learning and language, whereas the adult who intervenes in the play may prevent the child from being creative. Intervention is only necessary if the play becomes dangerous or too repetitive. There should be enough material provided for the entire group to take part in the activity, though not necessarily all at once.

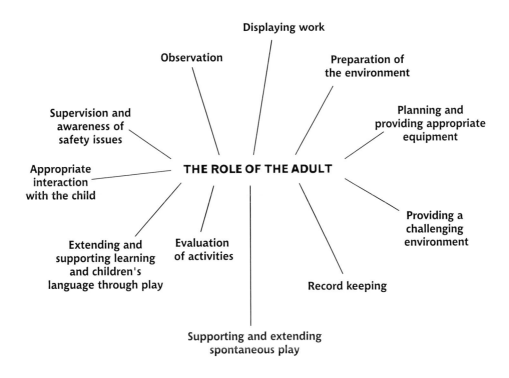

Displaying work

Observation

Preparation of the environment

Supervision and awareness of safety issues

Planning and providing appropriate equipment

Appropriate interaction with the child

THE ROLE OF THE ADULT

Providing a challenging environment

Extending and supporting learning and children's language through play

Evaluation of activities

Record keeping

Supporting and extending spontaneous play

There has to be enough space for the children, and they should have the chance to do the activity if they want. Young children should never be forced into doing an activity if they do not wish to. On the other hand, a child who refuses at first might well want to join in later on.

There is also the question of enough time. It is obviously not sensible to start a creative art activity that will take about an hour or more, just before the dinner break. You will also have to fit in with the time that your **supervisor** has given you.

All activities need to be supervised for safety reasons. Even playing with water can lead to a slippery floor and an unnecessary accident. Other activities, such as woodwork, cooking and outside play, have obvious built-in hazards, and need to be carefully planned and closely supervised. If there are small babies or toddlers in your establishment, even more care must be taken. Small beads or broken Lego bricks need to be put out of the way, to avoid choking accidents. Scissors, needles and knives should never be used or left lying around near babies or toddlers.

All the activities you plan need to be suitable and accessible to all the children in your care. All the resources you use need to be checked so that they promote **positive images** of all ethnic groups and cultures, and both genders. If you are not careful, you will find boys dominating the outside play, whilst the girls take over the role play corner. This is not acceptable, and you may need to make sure that all children can take part in all activities. If you have children with disabilities in your establishment, you must make sure that they have access to all activities.

Whatever the activity, the adult is there as a resource, to provide materials, time and space, and to take part when necessary. For example, in imaginary play, the adult should only take part if invited, whereas in cooking the presence of the adult is essential, in providing support, instructions and supervision.

Activities

- List three activities where adults would need to be involved for safety reasons and three where the presence of an adult is essential in extending the play.
- In your group, discuss any examples of adult intervention you have observed that you may have thought to be inappropriate.

The Early Years Foundation Stage

Since September 2008 *The Early Years Foundation Stage* (EYFS) has been mandatory for:

- all schools
- all early years providers in Ofsted registered settings.

It applies to children from birth to the end of the academic year in which the child has their fifth birthday.

In the *Statutory Framework for the Early Years Foundation Stage* the Department for Education and Skills tells us that:

> Every child deserves the best possible start in life and support to fulfil their potential. A child's experience in the early years has a major impact on their future life chances. A secure, safe and happy childhood is important in its own right, and it provides the foundation for children to make the most of their abilities and talents as they grow up. When parents choose to use early years services they want to know that provision will keep their children safe and help them to thrive. The Early Years Foundation Stage (EYFS) is the framework that provides that assurance. The overarching aim of the EYFS is to help young children achieve the five Every Child Matters outcomes...

Every Child Matters is the government agenda which focuses on bringing together services to support children and families. It sets out five major outcomes for children:

- being healthy
- staying safe
- enjoying and achieving
- making a positive contribution
- economic well-being.

The EYFS aims to meet the *Every Child Matters* outcomes by:

- **Setting standards** for the learning, development and care young children should experience when they attend a setting outside their family home. Every child should make progress, with no children left behind.
- **Providing equality of opportunity and anti-discriminatory practice.** Ensuring that every child is included and not disadvantaged because of ethnicity, culture, religion, home language, family background, learning difficulties or disabilities, gender or ability.
- **Creating a framework for partnership working between parents and professionals**, and between all the settings that the child attends.
- **Improving quality and consistency in the early years** through standards that apply to all settings. This provides the basis for the inspection and regulation regime carried out by Ofsted.
- **Laying a secure foundation for future learning** through learning and development that is planned around the individual needs and interests of the child. This is informed by the use of on-going observational assessment.

Note: The EYFS replaces *The Curriculum Guidance for the Foundation Stage, the Birth to Three Matters Framework* and *The National Standards for Under 8s Daycare and Childminding*, which are now defunct.

Themes, principles and commitments

The EYFS is based around four **themes**. Each theme is linked to a **principle**. Each principle is supported by four **commitments**. The commitments describe how their principle can be put into action. The themes, principles and commitments are shown in the table on page 9.

Additional statements are provided within the EYFS to explain each Commitment in more detail. You can see these on the Department for Education and Skills 'Principles into Practice' poster, an extract of which is reproduced below.

Theme	Principle	Commitments
1. A Unique Child	Every child is a competent learner from birth who can be resilient, capable, confident and self-assured.	1.1 Child development 1.2 Inclusive practice 1.3 Keeping safe 1.4 Health and well-being
2. Positive Relationships	Children learn to be strong and independent from a base of loving and secure relationships with parents and/or a key person.	2.1 Respecting each other 2.2 Parents as partners 2.3 Supporting learning 2.4 Key person
3. Enabling Environments	The environment plays a key role in supporting and extending children's development and learning.	3.1 Observation, assessment and planning 3.2 Supporting every child 3.3 The learning environment 3.4 The wider context
4. Learning and Development	Children develop and learn in different ways and at different rates. All areas of learning and development are equally important and interconnected.	4.1 Play and exploration 4.2 Active learning 4.3 Creativity and critical thinking 4.4 Areas of learning and development

Areas of learning and development

Theme 4, Learning and Development, also contains six areas of learning and development. These are shown on the diagram below:

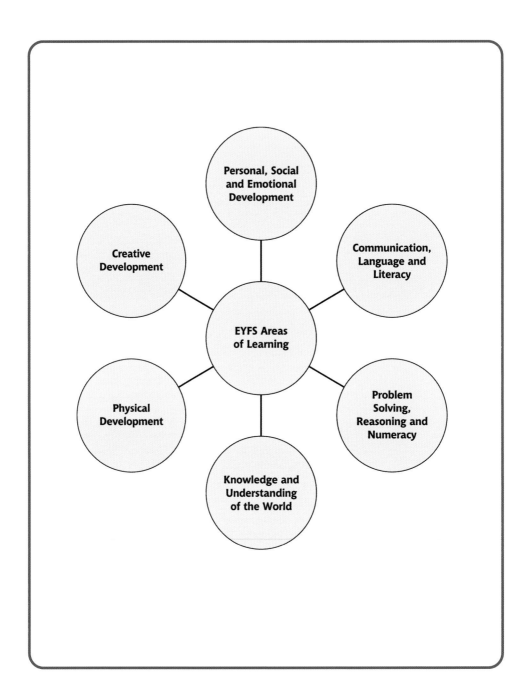

Each area of learning and development is divided up into aspects. You can see these on the Department for Education and Skills Learning and Development card, reproduced below. Together, the six areas of learning and development make up the skills, knowledge and experiences appropriate for babies and children as they grow, learn and develop. Although these are presented as separate areas, it's important to remember that for children everything links and nothing is compartmentalised. All areas of learning and development are connected to one another and are equally important. They are underpinned by the principles of the EYFS. Each area of learning also has a list of **early learning goals** (elg). The aim is for children to reach the goals by the end of their Reception year.

As you'll read below, there are a set of EYFS resource cards for practitioners. This includes a card for each area of learning which provides guidance on what practitioners must do to promote children's development, and outlines what this means to children.

Welfare requirements

Settings must also meet the EYFS welfare requirements in addition to the learning and development requirements. The welfare requirements fall into the following five categories:

Safeguarding and promoting children's welfare

- The provider must take necessary steps to safeguard and promote the welfare of children.
- The provider must promote the good health of the children, take necessary steps to prevent the spread of infection, and take appropriate action when they are ill.
- Children's behaviour must be managed effectively and in a manner appropriate for their stage of development and particular individual needs.

Suitable people

- Providers must ensure that adults looking after children, or having unsupervised access to them, are suitable to do so.
- Adults looking after children must have appropriate qualifications, training, skills and knowledge.
- Staffing arrangements must be organised to ensure safety and to meet the needs of the children.

Suitable premises, environment and equipment

- Outdoor and indoor spaces, furniture, equipment and toys must be safe and suitable for their purpose.

Organisation

- Providers must plan and organise their systems to ensure that every child receives an enjoyable and challenging learning and development experience that is tailored to meet their individual needs.

Documentation

- Providers must maintain records, policies and procedures required for the safe and efficient management of the settings and to meet the needs of the children.

So what does all this mean?

Childcarers working in settings following the EYFS need to meet the standards for learning, development and care. Their responsibilities include:

- planning a range of play and learning experiences that promote all of the aspects within all of the areas of learning
- assessing and monitoring individual children's progress through observational assessments
- using the findings of observational assessments to inform the planning of play and learning experiences
- ensuring that children's individual interests and abilities are promoted within the play and learning experiences.

In their 'Key Elements of Effective Practice' (KEEP) The Department for Education and Skills tells us that:

Effective practice in the early years requires committed, enthusiastic and reflective practitioners with a breadth and depth of knowledge, skills and understanding. Effective practitioners use their own learning to improve their work with young children and their families in ways which are sensitive, positive and non-judgemental. Therefore through initial and on-going training and development practitioners need to develop, demonstrate and continuously improve their:

- relationships with both children and adults
- understanding of the individual and diverse ways that children learn and develop
- knowledge and understanding in order to actively support and extend children's learning in and across all areas and aspects of learning and development
- practice in meeting all children's needs, learning styles and interests
- work with parents, carers and the wider community
- work with other professionals within and beyond the setting.

EYFS resources for childcarers

The EYFS pack of resources for providers includes:

The statutory framework for the Early Years Foundation Stage

This booklet sets out:

- the welfare requirements. *Which set out providers' duties to ensure children's welfare and well-being within the setting.*
- the learning and development requirements. *Which set out providers' duties under each of the six areas of learning and development.*

Practice guidance for the Early Years Foundation Stage

This booklet provides further guidance on:

- legal requirements
- the areas of learning and development
- the EYFS principles
- assessment.

24 cards

Which give the principles and commitments at a glance, with guidance on putting the principles into practice. They include an overview of child development.

CD-ROM

Which contains all the information from the booklets and cards. It includes information on effective practice, research and resources. This can also be accessed via the EYFS website (www.standards.dcsf.gov.uk/eyfs/). It's a good idea to take the overview tour to familiarise yourself with the site on your first visit. You can then follow the links to the areas of learning, and read more about the aspects, then follow the links to the 'Principles in practice' for examples of how practitioners following the EYFS work with children within their settings.

How does the EYFS apply to babies and toddlers?

As mentioned, the EYFS was introduced in 2008, and it applies to all children from birth to the end of the academic year in which they have their fifth birthday. Prior to this, there was a curriculum known as the Foundation Stage, which applied to children aged three to five years, and a separate framework (the 'Birth to Three Matters' framework) for younger children. So when learners are first introduced to the EYFS, they sometimes become a little confused.

The curriculum

Most can see how the themes, principles and commitments (see the table on page 9) apply to children of all ages. But they cannot always see immediately how the areas of learning and the aspects they are broken into (see pages 10–11) can apply to such a broad age range. However, there is an individual, double-sided resource card for each of the areas of learning which provides important information.

The card for personal, social and emotional development has been reproduced here. On side one, you'll find the requirements for personal, social and emotional development. This concisely tells providers what they must do to promote this area of learning. You'll see that each aspect of personal, social and emotional development has been expressed in more detail, and there's also a section which explains what personal, social and emotional development means for children. Take some time to study side one of the resource card now, remembering that babies and children will progressively work towards the aspirations that are listed for their development throughout their first five years.

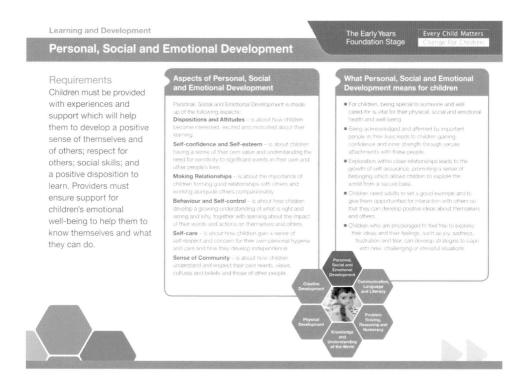

We'll consider how some of the information given on side one of the card relates to children of all ages. For instance:

- You will know about bonding between babies and their parents and the importance of babies forming key relationships with carers. So you'll see how being special to someone is as important to young babies as it is to older children.
- Growth of self-assurance should ideally begin when children are very young and carry on throughout their life, although this will be displayed in different ways at different ages, as highlighted in the following example.

Activity

Elliot's self-assurance grows

Elliot attends a day nursery. When he was 11 months old, Carolina was his baby room keyworker. She often sat on the carpet and played with Elliot. He would eventually crawl off to explore the room and resources available, but he would frequently return to the security of being by Carolina's side.

When he was two, Elliot moved to the toddler room. Carolina accompanied him on visits at first to help him to settle in and get to know his new keyworker, Mo. Mo supported Elliot as he got to know the other children. Before long, Mo and Elliot's family helped him to become toilet trained.

Now Elliot is three and he's starting to think of things to tell the whole group at circle time. He sometimes gets frustrated when he needs to wait for his turn, particularly when another child has a toy that he'd like. But with support Elliot is learning about feelings and how to cope with them.

- Was Carolina effectively promoting Elliot's development in the area of personal, social and emotional development? Give reasons for your answer.
- Is Elliot's personal, social and emotional development being promoted effectively now? Give reasons for your answer.

Side two of the resource card tells practitioners what areas they should give particular focus to in order to give all children the best opportunities for effective personal, social and emotional development. These are presented in the form of the EYFS themes and principles. Read them carefully now.

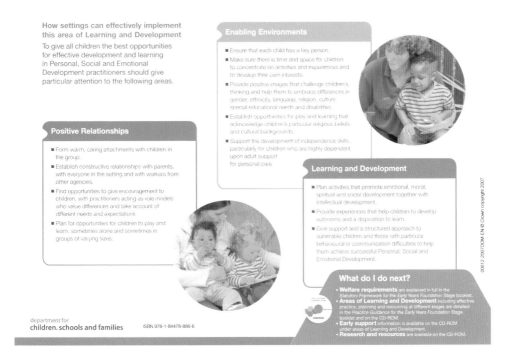

Returning to the practical example, which of the principles do you think Carolina and Mo were promoting in their work with Elliot? Hopefully, you've spotted several, although obviously the practitioners would be doing much more than just the brief example of practice given here.

Problem solving, reasoning and numeracy

Study the resource card for problem solving, reasoning and numeracy, which is reproduced on the next page.

Problem Solving, Reasoning and Numeracy

Requirements

Children must be supported in developing their understanding of Problem Solving, Reasoning and Numeracy in a broad range of contexts in which they can explore, enjoy, learn, practise and talk about their developing understanding. They must be provided with opportunities to practise these skills and to gain confidence and competence in their use.

Aspects of Problem Solving, Reasoning and Numeracy

Problem Solving, Reasoning and Numeracy is made up of the following aspects:

Numbers as Labels and for Counting – is about how children gradually know and use numbers and counting in play, and eventually recognise and use numbers reliably, to develop mathematical ideas and to solve problems.

Calculating – is about how children develop an awareness of the relationship between numbers and amounts and know that numbers can be combined to be 'added together' and can be separated by 'taking away' and that two or more amounts can be compared.

Shape, Space and Measures – is about how through talking about shapes and quantities, and developing appropriate vocabulary, children use their knowledge to develop ideas and to solve mathematical problems.

What Problem Solving, Reasoning and Numeracy means for children

- Babies' and children's mathematical development occurs as they seek patterns, make connections and recognise relationships through finding out about and working with numbers and counting, with sorting and matching and with shape, space and measures.
- Children use their knowledge and skills in these areas to solve problems, generate new questions and make connections across other areas of Learning and Development.

How settings can effectively implement this area of Learning and Development

To give all children the best opportunities for effective development and learning in Problem Solving, Reasoning and Numeracy practitioners should give particular attention to the following areas.

Enabling Environments

- Recognise the mathematical potential of the outdoor environment, for example, for children to discover things about shape, distance and measures, through their physical activity.
- Exploit the mathematical potential of the indoor environment, for example, enabling children to discover things about numbers, counting and calculating through practical situations such as finding out how many children are in the music area or how many story books a child has looked at today.
- Ensure that mathematical resources are readily available both indoors and outside.

Positive Relationships

- Give children sufficient time, space and encouragement to discover and use new words and mathematical ideas, concepts and language during child-initiated activities in their own play.
- Encourage children to explore real-life problems, to make patterns and to count and match together, for example, ask, "How many spoons do we need for everyone in this group to have one?".
- Support children who use a means of communication other than spoken English to develop and understand specific mathematical language while valuing knowledge of Problem Solving, Reasoning and Numeracy in the language or communication system that they use at home.
- Value children's own graphic and practical explorations of Problem Solving, Reasoning and Numeracy.

Learning and Development

- Develop mathematical understanding through all children's early experiences including through stories, songs, games and imaginative play.
- Provide a range of activities, some of which focus on mathematical learning and some which enable mathematical learning to be drawn out, for example, exploring shape, size and pattern during block play.
- Use mathematical terms during play and daily routines.

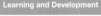

What do I do next?

- **Welfare requirements** are explained in full in the *Statutory Framework for the Early Years Foundation Stage* booklet.
- **Areas of Learning and Development** including effective practice, planning and resourcing at different stages are detailed in the *Practice Guidance for the Early Years Foundation Stage* booklet and on the CD-ROM.
- **Early Support** information is available on the CD-ROM under areas of Learning and Development.
- **Research and resources** are available on the CD-ROM.

department for
children. schools and families   ISBN 978-1-84478-886-6

00012-2007DOM-EN © Crown copyright 2007

Hopefully you are beginning to see how problem solving, reasoning and numeracy can be promoted for babies and young children, as well as for older children. It's all a matter of providing activities and experiences that are appropriate to children's level. So a toddler may play with a shape sorter, while a four year old may draw shapes in the sand with her finger. The older child may independently count out how many knives and forks are needed at lunch time, while the toddler may follow a request to 'give one to everyone'.

You can view all of the learning and development resource cards online at www.standards.dcsf.gov.uk/eyfs/site/resource/pdfs.htm.

The National Curriculum

For information about the National Curriculum, which applies to children aged 5–16 years, see Chapter 18.

The 'Children's Plan'

In 2007, the government published the 'Children's Plan' which sets out ambitious new goals for 2020. The Plan is intended to:

- strengthen support for all families during the formative early years of their children's lives
- take the next steps in achieving world class schools and an excellent education for every child
- involve parents fully in their children's learning
- help to make sure that young people have interesting and exciting things to do outside of school
- provide more places for children to play safely.

There will be regular reports on the progress the government is making. For more information, visit www.dfes.gov.uk/publications/childrensplan/.

Evaluating performance

As a professional person you will become adept at evaluating your own performance and practice. When working with children from birth to 7:11 years this includes planning and preparing all the activities you undertake with the children, and evaluating the success or otherwise of the play experience. To help you do this, use the evaluation chart on page 183.

Monitoring for anti-discriminatory practice

You will become more and more aware, during your course, of the rights of all children and their families to equality of opportunity, and the importance of anti-discriminatory practice. The chart for monitoring anti-discriminatory practice on page 184 will help you ensure that the activities you are providing meet the individual needs of all the children, and you may find it useful to use this from time to time to monitor your perception and sensitivity in this area.

National Vocational Qualifications

Many of you using this book may be working towards acquiring National Vocational Qualifications (NVQs) in Children's Care, Learning and Development, either at Level 2 or Level 3. There are mandatory and optional units at each level. NVQs are designed mainly for people already working with children, who wish to be assessed by an NVQ assessor on their performance and practice according to the prescribed standards. Candidates are expected to demonstrate underpinning knowledge and understanding of childcare and education.

Resources

Brown B., 1998, *Unlearning Discrimination in the Early Years*, Trentham Books.

Dare A. et al, 2009, *A Practical Guide to Working with Babies*, 4th edition, Nelson Thornes.

The Statutory Framework for the Early Years Foundation Stage, Department for Children, Schools and Families.

Websites

www.blss.portsmouth.sch.uk/earlyyears

http://teachersnet.net/gazette

www.onlineplaygroup.com

www.standards.dcsf.gov.uk/eyfs/

www.everychildmatters.gov.uk

www.direct.gov.uk

www.qca.org.uk

www.pre-school.org.uk

www.ndna.org.uk

www.ncma.org.uk

Part 2

Activities for Babies and Toddlers

For babies and toddlers, play is just as important as it is for older children. It is sometimes not fully realised that babies need activities and a bored baby may become an unhappy baby. Some babies may cry when they do not have enough to do, and a stimulating activity will distract the baby, and has more value than a pacifier, such as a rocking chair or a dummy.

This part of the book looks at the need for stimulation of very young children, and how best to offer a variety of activities to babies and toddlers. The chapters point out good practice and emphasise how crucial safety is with the youngest children.

2 Activities with Babies

Babies are learning and developing from the moment of conception. The newborn baby quickly learns to recognise the face, the smell, the feel, the taste and the voice of the mother, thus using all the senses to ensure survival.

Development

In addition to love, protection, shelter and food, the baby also needs stimulation. At first the mother provides all the stimulation the baby requires, through gentle handling and stroking, speaking in a soft voice and feeding on demand.

As the baby develops, the interaction between the mother or main caregiver and the baby becomes increasingly important. The baby's routine becomes more established, and there is time to play when feeding, bathing and changing nappies. Many babies are spending larger parts of the day awake, and this is a time to truly interact, and to ensure that the baby is not left alone and bored.

Encouraging development

By six weeks, most babies are smiling, showing that they are responding to a **stimulus**, usually during a conversation whilst maintaining good eye contact. This is the time to introduce other stimuli, such as mobiles and rattles. The mobiles that will interest the baby most will have the pictures positioned so that the baby can gaze at them when lying on her back in the crib or cot, or in a bouncing cradle. Bright colours add interest, and some have a musical attachment. They can be bought or home made. Babies also learn by taking all objects to their mouths, so rattles and other toys must be carefully checked for safety: durable, well made, non-toxic, no sharp edges and impossible to swallow.

By far the most important stimulus is still the consistent contact given to the baby by parents, siblings, grandparents and other familiar adults. Interacting with songs and cuddles and talking to the baby will aid emotional, intellectual and language development. The first response will be facial – smiles and intense looks. Be sure to take turns, and listen to the baby when she begins to vocalise.

After changing the baby's nappy, allow some time for play with hands and feet, unrestricted by clothing. Most babies enjoy their bathtimes, getting pleasure from the warmth of the water, and the freedom to kick and splash. This aids all-round development.

Activity

Describe in detail the areas of development that are extended by bathtime.

At around six weeks, babies can be seen occasionally moving their hands towards objects in their field of vision, and sometimes accidentally succeeding in touching them. At three months, babies discover their hands and begin to engage in finger play. By six months, this area of **hand–eye coordination** is usually well established and babies can reach out for an object they desire, and grasp it. Initially, toys such as activity centres, which hang suspended just within the baby's reach, will help develop this skill. Playmats with a range of different sensory activities will help stimulate the baby's interest.

Increasingly, the baby's responses are no longer just **reflex** reactions to **sensory** stimuli, but become selective, choosing which stimulus to react to. Lightweight rattles and toys that can be easily held in the hand help to develop hand–eye coordination.

When the baby is able to sit up with support, other toys can be offered. The baby will enjoy knocking down towers built of plastic or foam bricks, banging saucepans and lids with a wooden spoon and having fun with weighted or suction toys that stay within the baby's reach.

Singing to the baby comes naturally to most parents and caregivers. From action songs to finger rhymes, from nursery rhymes to lullabies, babies will get pleasure from them all, and enjoy a sense of security and comfort. Singing helps babies to discriminate sounds and anticipate repetitive actions.

Reading to a small baby sometimes seems rather odd, but the baby will enjoy the close contact, and start to recognise familiar objects seen in picture books. It is a useful introduction to the world of books and exposure to 'book' language.

Some very simple games are enjoyable to play with very young babies. Lying the baby on a playmat or bean bag, you might:

- make eye contact with the baby, take the baby's hands and let the baby feel your face whilst you talk and sing
- hold an object in front of the baby, and move it from side to side, encouraging the baby to follow it. From about six weeks encourage the baby to reach out for the object, remembering to talk and praise the baby
- move the baby's legs in a cycling motion
- clap the baby's hands together
- massage and stroke the baby.

Other activities to stimulate the baby include:

- playing 'Peek-a-boo'
- placing the baby on her tummy, and placing toys in front of her to encourage head control at first, and movement at a later stage.

Emotional development

Some babies are very demanding of attention, and cry each time they are left on their own, whilst others settle quite happily by themselves, perhaps playing with their hands or feet. All babies should be picked up when they cry and never left to 'cry it out'. Less demanding babies also need attention and stimulating play activities should be offered. Babies need to make close emotional attachments and, if in day care, should be cared for by as few people as possible, ideally by a **key worker**. The parents will tell you which songs, activities and rhymes the baby enjoys.

Intellectual development

Babies develop intelligence mainly through their senses. Once babies are mobile, curiosity about their environment is paramount, and they should be allowed to explore as much as they wish, always ensuring they are safe and not exposed to hazards. Continually talking and listening to babies' **vocalisations** helps encourage early language development, and the first words may start to appear at the end of the first year.

Becoming mobile

During the first year of life, the baby will have developed physical control, sitting first with and then without support, rolling, creeping and crawling, pulling to stand and taking the first few hand-held steps. Some may be walking confidently by their first birthday, whilst others may need encouragement to get started, and there are many toys you can provide, such as baby walkers, trucks and trolleys, which can be pushed along. The types of walkers in which you sit the baby are unsafe and have been known to cause accidents.

Encouraging sensory development

The treasure basket

All areas of sensory development can be encouraged by the use of a treasure basket, as described by Elinor Goldschmied. The baby is offered a container filled with objects made of natural materials, none of them plastic or recognisable as 'toys'.

Amount of space	Type of space		Type of play		Adult involvement
Whole area	Outside	✔	Solitary	✔	Essential
Half area	Inside	✔	Parallel		Enriching
Quarter area	Hard surface		Small group		Not always necessary
Small area ✔	Carpeted	✔	Large group		
	Table space				Can be intrusive ✔

Essential materials for the treasure basket
- Container, preferably a basket, large enough to hold at least 20 items.
- Cushion or bean bag, in order to support the baby comfortably on the floor.
- Rug, if used outside.
- About 20 items to stimulate the five senses, such as a plastic baby-mirror, an orange, a fir cone, a piece of pumice, a small natural sponge, tissue paper, a large stone, small cloth bags containing lavender or cloves, a brush, a piece of velvet, clothes pegs and a bunch of keys.

Suggested additional equipment
- Any natural object, as long as it is safe for the baby to play with.

There is an excellent chapter in *People Under Three* by Elinor Goldschmied and Sonia Jackson, giving many further suggestions.

Activity

Plan a treasure basket. List five items for each of the senses.

✓ Good practice: role of the adult when using a treasure basket

- All the equipment must be kept clean and perishable objects such as fruit need to be discarded and replaced as necessary.
- The baby should be allowed to explore the items without any adult intervention or encouragement. Adults should supervise from a distance and not talk or interact with the baby, as this will interfere with the baby's concentration.
- Items should be changed or washed fairly often so as to continually stimulate exploratory play.
- A comfortable and safe position for the baby must be found, so that the baby does not topple over and become distracted.
- If the baby is using the basket among a group of older, mobile children, care must be taken to ensure that the older children do not spoil the activity by handling or taking away the objects. A heavy stone, for example, whilst pleasant for the baby to touch, might turn into a lethal weapon in the hands of an older child.

Activity

Visit a good toy shop. Make a note of toys that would extend each area of development for a six month old and for an 11 month old.

Essential points

Anti-discriminatory practice

- Babies could be introduced to exotic smells, objects and materials from all around the world.
- The treasure basket is a gender-free activity.
- Older children with special needs, who are unable to move around freely, will gain stimulation from a treasure basket.
- The individual needs of the baby should be discussed with the parent and incorporated into any activity.

Safety

- Care must be taken when selecting the items for the treasure basket, checking to see that there are no sharp edges, nothing is too heavy, and nothing small enough to swallow or insert into noses and ears.
- All toys and equipment given to a baby should be clean and need to be washable to avoid infection. They should be durable to avoid accidents from broken edges, and only non-toxic paint should be used. They should conform to safety standards.
- Small babies are vulnerable to suffocation, so avoid using pillows and cushions, and ensure that any plastic bags are stored out of the baby's reach.
- Anything with strings should not be near the baby as, if the string becomes wrapped around the neck or other parts of the body, the blood supply could be cut off, or the child could be hanged.
- Be careful with heavy objects near the baby.
- Always supervise floor play.
- Make sure the baby's environment is clean, safe and hazard free.

Partnership with parents

- **If you are working with babies you need to involve parents as much as you can in their baby's day.**
- **Parents must feel confident that their child is safe and happy.**
- **A key worker system should be in place, so that parents and babies have one main person with whom to relate.**
- **Information should be shared at the start and end of each day, and this will include details of the activities that have been carried out.**

Resources

Emerson S., 1992, *Baby Games and Lullabies*, Kingfisher Books.

Goldschmied E. and Jackson S., 2003, *People Under Three*, 2nd edition, RoutledgeFalmer.

Manning-Morton J. and Thorp M., 2006, *Key Times: A framework for developing high quality provision for children from birth to three*, OUP.

Miller L., 1992, *Understanding Your Baby*, Rosendale Press.

Murray L. and Andrews L., 2005, *The Social Baby: Understanding Babies' Communication from Birth*, CP Publishing.

Sheridan M. et al, 2007, *From Birth to Five Years: Children's Developmental Progress*, 3rd edition, Routledge.

Silberg J., 2004, *Games to Play with Babies*, 3rd edition, Brilliant Publications.

Woolfson R., 2003, *Bright Start: understand and stimulate your child's development from birth to five years*, Hamlyn.

Websites

www.peep.org.uk

www.standards.dcsf.gov.uk/eyfs/

www.everychildmatters.gov.uk

www.pre-school.org.uk

www.ndna.org.uk

www.ncma.org.uk

3 Activities with Toddlers

When working with toddlers, you will find it useful to look at each area of development and the activities and toys that will help promote and extend this development.

Development

Toddlers are challenging, and often the toys and activities provided by the adults may be used in a very different way by the child from that expected by the adult, but this is acceptable as learning is taking place, and toddlers should be given every opportunity to explore and set their own agenda within a safe environment.

Physical development

Encouraging gross motor skills (large body movements)

Balls of all sizes, made out of various materials, stimulate a toddler to move, and extend the mobility of children who are already walking, aiding their balance and coordination. As the toddler becomes more proficient at walking, pull-along toys are fun and encourage children to walk for a longer period. Once children are mobile and walking confidently, the next stage is learning and practising skills and exploring the environment.

Suggestions for toddlers include a staircase on which they should be shown initially how to climb upstairs and, more importantly, how to crawl down; and a small slide to practise climbing skills. Sliding down is the reward!

'Hidey hole' boxes or large wooden cubes, which are sturdy and large enough for toddlers to climb in, promote skills of getting in and out of objects, coordination and balance. Strong supermarket cartons are an acceptable alternative.

Wheeled toys to sit on, and move with the feet, encourage the practice of steering skills, balance and coordination, and help to strengthen leg muscles.

A low climbing frame aids balance and coordination, and strengthens arm and leg muscles, as do balls, for throwing, catching and kicking.

Outings to parks, where the playground will have swings, seesaws, roundabouts and rocking toys, are enjoyable. Here, children can use the equipment according to their own individual skills, under close supervision.

Encouraging fine manipulative skills (small manipulative skills)

During the first year, babies start to practise the skills of handling and manipulating small objects, reaching and grasping, holding and letting go, moving objects from hand to hand, passing objects, poking and pointing with one finger, and picking up objects with finger and thumb. There are many materials that will help develop manipulative skills and hand–eye coordination, such as bricks for building towers that can be knocked down; stacking cups and beakers; small tins and cartons that can be improvised from around the house; posting boxes; hammer sets; dolls that are easily undressed; and simple inset jigsaws.

The contents of the lower kitchen cupboards, where it is sensible to store only safe sturdy equipment, such as saucepans, plastic storage containers, baking tins and wooden spoons, can be played with as well as small bouncy balls, Duplo, large threading toys such as cotton reels and large wooden beads, and screw toys. Play dough, crayons and finger paints can be used.

 Activity

Obtain catalogues from at least four different manufacturers, and select what seems to you to be the best outdoor equipment for a toddler, so as to promote all-round physical development.

Social and moral development

Up to the age of one year there is little social development, and no sign of any moral development, but as a foundation for moral development, the consistency and firmness of the caregivers in handling the behaviour of the toddler will ensure a good start.

During the second year, as the child becomes mobile and understands more, she has to learn how to fit happily into the family and the larger outside environment, and a whole set of rules has to be learnt about acceptable behaviour. At this stage, play is solitary, but the presence of a familiar adult provides reassurance and security. A toddler is not interested in playing cooperatively with other children. She has just learnt the meaning of 'mine', and the concept of sharing usually does not occur until the third year.

Encouraging social development

Introducing toddlers to the wider environment will help them come to terms with the outside world. Outings to visit the family, walks in the park, perhaps meeting other small children to play alongside, and leisurely expeditions to local shops where a conversation might take place, will all help toddlers understand their roles in the community.

Parent and toddler groups, toy libraries, visits to the local library, drop-in centres and clinics where other small children are likely to be found, will enlarge a toddler's social circle.

Provision of small-scale household equipment, such as brooms and vacuum cleaners, allows the toddler to imitate the parent, and encourages the beginning of role play.

Emotional development

During the first year, the baby has progressed emotionally from total dependency to an understanding that there are some things she is able to do on her own, and this increases with age. You will need to have patience as the toddler tries to help you with her own care or with the chores.

It is often possible to avoid confrontations, but if these do take place, toddlers are usually quite amenable to diversions. Some feelings are so strong and overpowering that you just have to wait until the storm has passed, and then cuddle and comfort the child, who may well be frightened by the immensity of these emotions. A great deal depends on the developing personality of the child, as to how happy or sad the child may be. Comfort objects, such as dummies, blankets, a special soft toy or any other item to which the child is particularly attached, play a large part in their lives, and no attempt should be made to remove them.

It is best to have as few rules as possible, and to make sure that the environment is safe and offers security.

Although toddlers are stepping out into the wider world, they still need the love and support of a familiar adult, and find new emotional demands difficult to deal with. You need to be aware of this when first building a relationship with any child, and proceed slowly and sensitively.

Encouraging emotional development

Messy play, such as finger painting or play with wet clay, dough, water, wet sand, mud or cooked pasta, will soothe upset children and allow an outlet for aggressive feelings.

Activity

Mix some cornflour with a little water and let the toddlers smooth it on to the table and roll it in their hands. Observe what happens, and record their reactions.

Outings and vigorous play outside help children to release pent-up feelings and tire them out, so that they will sleep better at night. Bathtimes help children to unwind at the end of the day.

If you give time for toddlers to feed themselves and let them help to dress and undress themselves, you will find that they soon become quite skilled.

Toddlers can start to make decisions, but it is best just to give them only two choices, such as 'Would you like to paint or play in the garden?'

Intellectual and language development

Children learn at an amazing rate and, during the first year, the baby has learnt, among other things, to become mobile, to understand a great deal of what is said, to speak a few words, to identify people they are in regular contact with and to recognise food they enjoy. The next years show an acceleration of learning as the toddler becomes more proficient with language. Although play is mainly solitary, the toddler spends an increasingly large proportion of time in exploratory and experimental play, in looking at books, listening to and taking part in songs and rhymes, learning that objects have names, as do parts of the body, and realising that by using language, needs are met without having recourse to pointing and crying.

Encouraging intellectual and language development

The child should have access to a good selection of picture books, many of which can be handled alone, and the adult needs to have a range of finger plays, songs, action rhymes, nursery rhymes and verse.

Opportunities should be found for conversation and good communication, taking time to listen as well as talk. Providing interest tables, displaying pictures and posters, and allowing toddlers to handle objects; all these things will stimulate their curiosity, as well as helping to extend their vocabulary. You will need to gain a sound theoretical understanding of language acquisition to ensure you promote this important area of development.

There are many toys on the market for children of this age. The most essential are bricks and blocks. (Duplo, foam blocks and plastic bricks do less harm than wooden ones if thrown around.) Posting boxes and similar toys encourage hand–eye coordination, memory and concentration.

Children gain a great deal of pleasure and learning from bath toys, where early concepts of floating, sinking, volume and capacity may be learnt.

Small-scale domestic equipment, such as telephones, brooms and tea sets, can be provided to encourage imitative play.

Activity

Visit a good bookshop and list the books suitable to extend the language of a 15 month old and a two year old.

Heuristic play

This type of play was devised by Elinor Goldschmied for groups of toddlers and is particularly suitable for children in day care. It is intended as an enrichment of the children's play and the staff need to be committed to carrying it out on a regular basis.

Fifteen bags are provided, and each bag should have enough of the same objects for all the children in the group. The contents might include bulldog clips, corks, springs, curlers, short pieces of chain, old keys, cardboard tubes, extra large curtain rings, tins and lids, small boxes and anything else that a toddler would safely enjoy exploring. Receptacles should be provided for the children to collect the items if they so wish.

The role of the adult is to provide the objects and keep them clean and in good order. They should not participate in the play in any way, but just sit quietly at the side of the room, which has been emptied of all furniture and equipment. The children enter this empty space and start exploring the objects in the bags. The activity can go on for 40 minutes, thoroughly engrossing the children in the same way that the treasure basket does for less mobile children. Toddlers have an increasing desire to explore and experiment, and heuristic play satisfies this need. Workers in day care centres are enthusiastic about heuristic play, as it is seen to be satisfying and enjoyable for the toddlers, and allows the adults to observe the development of the children.

Sensory development

Very young children learn mainly through their senses. As they grow older, learning in this way becomes less dominant. Toddlers, not yet in full command of language, use all their senses spontaneously in exploratory and experimental play. It is important that carers ensure children's safety, but toddlers should not be discouraged from exploring things through their senses when it is safe for them to do so. For instance, it is natural and instinctive for babies and toddlers to take objects to their mouth, and to touch things that interest them. Children who have a sensory impairment should be encouraged to use their senses in their play, and appropriate resources and experiences should be provided to support their development.

Activity

It's important that you offer inclusive activities. What steps could you take to ensure:

- That a toddler with a hearing impairment has the opportunity to enjoy nursery rhymes and songs?
- That a toddler with a visual impairment has opportunities to explore their creativity?
- That a toddler with a physical impairment who is not expected to stand or walk has opportunities to practise (other) gross motor movements?

Good practice: role of the adult

- Encourage toddlers to enjoy and take part in movement, songs and creative physical play, for example rolling on the floor, bouncing and splashing in puddles.
- Provide sensory play, such as feely boxes, handling natural materials, clay, water and sand.
- Provide resources to support imaginative play, such as large boxes, role play corners, dressing up clothes.
- Make sure there are links to home in some of the activities, providing resources such as pans, telephones and computers.
- Try to provide space for quiet play.
- Make time to talk and listen to the toddler.
- Toddlers need time to learn new skills and make connections: do not rush new learning and allow for repetition.

Essential points

Anti-discriminatory practice

- With the toddler's increasing understanding of language, it is important that you choose books that show positive images of all cultures, of both sexes, and show disabled people in leading roles.
- At this age, children start to realise what gender they are, and this is important to them. Toddlers should be encouraged to play with all toys and try out every type of activity, and not just provided with toys and activities thought to be suitable for one gender only.

▶

- The individual needs of the toddler should be identified with the parent and incorporated into any activities.

Safety
- Toddlers always need to be closely supervised. Their natural curiosity and adventurousness will lead them into potentially dangerous activities, so their environment needs to be as hazard-free as possible.
- All toys and equipment need to be durable and bought from a reputable manufacturer, and need to be checked for damage, maintained and repaired if necessary.
- Make sure that anything they are playing with cannot be swallowed or inserted into ears or up noses.

With the beginning of language, toddlers will understand when you say no, and you can start to teach them the rules of safety, but remember that understanding these rules will relate to the age and stage of development of the child. Remember to:

- provide safety gates on stairs and at the entrance to the kitchen
- provide fixed fire and cooker guards
- provide plug guards
- ensure harmful substances, such as bleach and medication, are locked up out of reach
- ensure gates and doors to the outside are locked
- ensure the child cannot lock herself in the freezer, fridge, bathroom, garden shed or any area where there may be danger
- use a harness in pram, high-chair and pushchair
- use reins in the street
- never leave a baby or toddler alone in the bath or the car or outside a shop
- never leave hot drinks within reach of a baby or a toddler.

Partnership with parents

- **Information should be shared at the beginning and the end of every day.**
- **Exchange games and ideas for activities with parents.**

Resources

Beswick C., 2003, *100 Language Games for Ages 0–3*, Scholastic.

Butler D., 1998, *Babies Need Books: Sharing the Joy of Books with Children from Birth to Six*, Revised edition, Butterworth-Heinemann.

Corbett P. and Emerson S., 1992, *Dancing and Singing Games*, Kingfisher Books.

Gee R. and Meredith S., 1993, *Entertaining and Educating Your Preschool Child*, Usborne Publishing.

Goldschmied E. and Hughes A., 1992, *Heuristic Play with Objects*, NCB.

Goldschmied E. and Jackson S., 2003, *People Under Three*, 2nd edition, RoutledgeFalmer.

Manning-Morton J. and Thorp M., 2006, *Key Times: A framework for developing high quality provision for children from birth to three*, OUP.

Post J. and Hohmann N., 2000, *Tender Care and Early Learning: supporting families and toddlers in childcare settings*, HighScope Press.

Sharp A., 2002, *100 Learning Games for Ages 0–3*, Scholastic.

Sharp P., 2001, *Nurturing Emotional Literacy*, Fulton.

Silberg J., 2005, *Games to Play with Toddlers*, 2nd edition, Brilliant Publications.

Silberg J., 2002, *Games to Play with Two-Year-Olds*, 2nd edition, Gryphon House Inc.

Thompson J., 2006, *Toddlercare*, Carroll & Brown Publishers Ltd.

Websites

www.zerotothree.org

www.raz-kids.com

Part 3

Activities for Young Children

The chapters in Part 3 look at a range of activities that are frequently enjoyed by children and that offer opportunities to promote their development and learning. After an introduction to the activity, we have looked at the amount and type of space needed to implement the activity successfully, the type of play and the amount of adult involvement required. We have listed the essential materials needed and suggested additional equipment that might extend the play.

We point out in these chapters the value of each activity to the children's development and learning, linked to the Early Years Foundation Stage and underpinned by anti-discriminatory practice and the need for safety. Most of the activities described are also suitable for babies, toddlers and the school-age child, with just the level of the involvement and supervision being different. Each chapter outlines the role of the adult, pointers for parents and concludes with a resources list.

4 Natural and Malleable Materials

Natural materials are readily available and very familiar. Water, sand, clay, mud and wood, unlike most materials provided for young children, cost very little or even nothing. Because of their familiarity, it is easy to involve children in planning their own experiences with natural materials, and asking them to decide what tools and equipment they wish to use.

Malleable materials include clay and mud and any other material that can be moulded in the same way, such as dough and plasticine. These materials can be used for modelling as well as providing **tactile** sensory experiences.

Water

Water is the most familiar of all the natural materials. Nearly all babies grow to love their bathtime, and the enjoyment of water is carried through to adulthood; swimming is a favourite leisure activity. Children find playing with water enjoyable and therapeutic. Water is an indestructible material and children can bang and splash without harm. It is as usual to find the quiet child at the water tray, playing contentedly on her own, as it is to find a noisy group using the equipment provided and finding out about floating and sinking. Playing with water links home and school. Children learn that water comes in many forms: as snow, rain, steam and ice, and is essential for life.

Amount of space		Type of space		Type of play		Adult involvement	
Whole area		Outside	✔	Solitary	✔	Essential	
Half area		Inside	✔	Parallel	✔	Enriching	✔
Quarter area		Hard surface	✔	Small group	✔	Not always necessary	✔
Small area	✔	Carpeted		Large group		Can be intrusive	
		Table space					

Essential materials

- Water of a tepid temperature
- Containers: a water tray; if in the child's home, a sink, basin, baby bath or the bath could be used

- Towel
- Protective clothing for children: aprons, sleeves, shower caps
- Floor mop.

Suggested additional equipment

- Colour: vegetable dyes, non-toxic powder paint
- Detergent for bubbles; pipes and tubing
- Dolls and dolls' clothes
- Sieves, plastic cartons with holes in
- Objects that float or sink: golf balls, stones, erasers, paper, etc.
- Graded vessels
- Decorators' brushes and small buckets for water painting
- Waterwheels and hoses
- Boats made in class
- Props for imaginative play, such as dinosaurs or toy fish
- Leaves, pieces of bark, shells, sponges, seaweed.

Links to the EYFS

Personal, social and emotional development

Children learn to take turns and share equipment, which leads to cooperation in other areas. They have to learn and accept certain safety rules. Playing in a small group is a social activity. Shy children can become involved at their own pace. Children find water play therapeutic, enjoyable, relaxing and calming.

Communication, language and literacy

Children will communicate needs and will become familiar with correct terminology, such as 'volume' and 'density'. They will explore new words particular to water, such as 'splish, splash'. They may discuss ideas and feelings, listen, talk and ask questions.

Problem solving, reasoning and numeracy

Using different equipment, many mathematical, scientific and technological concepts may be explored, such as floating and sinking and **conservation** of capacity and volume. Concentration is promoted as children often play with water for long periods of time. Decisions have to be made by the children.

Knowledge and understanding of the world

Children will watch the sun play on water. Looking at reflections, colours, bubbles and rainbows promotes an appreciation of the wonders of the natural ▷

world. They investigate the properties of different materials such as cork floating and stones sinking. Absorption is understood when children experiment with cotton wool and sponges.

Physical development

Lifting and pouring water develops arm muscles and hand–eye coordination. Picking up and placing equipment exercises manipulative skills and promotes correct use of tools.

Creative development

The properties of water are explored through varied sensory experiences: feeling the water, its movement and temperature; seeing the reflections, colours, bubbles and movements of the water and objects on or in it; and listening to the sounds of the water. It may lead to imaginary play.

Activity

Your supervisor in the nursery class has asked you to fill the water tray.

- **What should the temperature of the water be?**
- **List six objects you could put in the water to extend the play.**
- **How might you protect the children from getting wet?**
- **Name two hazards linked with water play.**

Good practice: role of the adult

- Water must be clean and of a pleasant temperature. It should be changed twice a day, and the temperature topped up. The equipment and tray need to be cleaned and washed regularly. The children could help with these tasks.
- Children must be protected. Keep the floor as dry as possible so that children do not slip and fall. Very young children must be carefully supervised and never left alone, as babies can drown in only a few centimetres of water. Fully cover clothing so that children do not get wet and chilled. Dry everyone's hands after play. Ensure children with eczema spend only a short time at the water tray and their hands and arms should be very carefully dried afterwards.

- Numbers must be limited to suit the size of the tray. This can easily be done by limiting the number of aprons available.
- The tray should be sited away from the quiet area, but within easy access of an adult, and near a water supply.
- All equipment should be in good condition and should be visible and accessible to the children. Labelling and classifying will aid the learning experience.
- The chosen activity should be age-appropriate. Children should be involved in choosing it and encouraged to experiment. There should be a good range of equipment to give the children the widest variety of experiences.
- Never fill the tray with tools and equipment, but make sure that there is enough for each child to use without too much turn-taking.
- Encourage children to be creative, asking **open-ended questions**, and helping them to investigate.
- Introduce language that is specific to learning in this area, using words such as 'siphon' and 'dissolve'.

Activity

List as many examples as you can of mathematical concepts that water play promotes, giving the equipment you would use to encourage each concept.

Sand

Sand is not found indoors in the home so it is generally less familiar to children than water, although some children do have sand pits in their gardens. Almost without exception, infant school classes, nurseries and playgroups will provide sand trays, and most will give the experience of wet and dry sand to the children.

Dry sand is relaxing and therapeutic to play with. A great deal can be learnt with the use of various tools. Dry sand is not suitable for very young children, unless closely supervised, as they tend to throw it around and get it in their eyes and hair as well as eat it.

Wet sand is suitable for all age groups. It can be used as a modelling material, and can be combined with blocks and cars and other small world toys to stimulate the imagination. It will lend itself to many mathematical, scientific and technological experiments.

Amount of space		Type of space		Type of play		Adult involvement	
Whole area		Outside	✔	Solitary	✔	Essential	
Half area		Inside	✔	Parallel	✔	Enriching	✔
Quarter area		Hard surface	✔	Small group	✔	Not always necessary	✔
Small area	✔	Carpeted		Large group	✔		
		Table space				Can be intrusive	✔

Essential materials

- Washed or silver sand, available from builders' merchants – check that no chemicals have been used
- Two containers, one for wet sand and one for dry sand
- Broom, dust pan and brush.

Suggested additional materials

- Similar tools and containers to those used for water play, with the addition of rakes, sand combs, scoops, etc.
- Natural materials, such as shells, pine cones, twigs, feathers and plants
- Shower cap to protect long or curly hair

- Buckets and spades, moulds, small world toys and vehicles
- Wooden blocks for ramps and buildings
- Flat trays for pattern making and early printing.

Links to the EYFS

Personal, social and emotional development

Sharing, planning and cooperating with other children are encouraged. Accepting and understanding the need for rules is reinforced.

A relaxing therapeutic activity, sand play allows for release of aggression. It is enjoyable and often associated with beach holidays or playing in the park and making new friends. There is no right or wrong way to use sand. It encourages cooperation and turn-taking.

Communication, language and literacy

Sand gives opportunities to express needs, communicate decisions and learn new vocabulary, with words such as 'gritty' or 'sifting'. Making patterns and marks in sand is linked to early literacy. Many conversations take place around the sand tray.

Problem solving, reasoning and numeracy

New concepts can be learnt (especially with the involvement of an adult and suitable equipment), such as light and heavy, full and empty. It is the perfect material for experimentation, exploration and aiding concentration, and leads to imaginative play.

Knowledge and understanding of the world

Sand makes links with the physical environment, and can be used in construction work, making homes and buildings. The wonder of the natural world can be appreciated with freedom to express creative ideas and feelings.

Physical development

Dry sand: pouring sand and filling containers develops arm muscles and hand–eye coordination. Dexterity is needed to handle tools correctly. Wet sand: control is needed when making moulds.

Creative development

Making patterns in sand is creative and aesthetic. The imagination is stimulated. Dry sand is a **tactile** experience, particularly digging your toes into an outside sand area. Children learn about the properties of sand through the senses, and particularly through touching it. Tasting should be discouraged at all costs!

✓ Good practice: role of the adult

- Sand must be kept clean. Outside, sand must be totally covered and the cover secured when not being used. If swept up from the floor, the sand must be washed thoroughly and all grit and dirt removed before being put back in the sand tray. To do this, place sand in container, pour on water to cover and the dirt will rise to the surface.
- Sand should be available every day, with the tools changed regularly so as to encourage and stimulate the creativity and imagination of the children.
- Adults should spend some time with the children at the sand tray so as to encourage appropriate language, investigation, estimating and **hypothesising**.
- It is sensible to site the indoor sand trays away from carpeted areas, so that spilt sand can be swept up easily. Adults and children should have ease of access to the sand.
- Adults need to supervise sand play to make sure that sand is not thrown. Children with long, oiled or very curly hair should be encouraged sensitively to tie it back, cover it with a scarf or wear a shower cap.
- Younger children need little or no tools in the sand, as they get great sensory enjoyment through using their hands to mould and feel the sand. When equipment is used for certain experiences, it needs to be part of the overall curriculum plan. There should also be some opportunity for children to choose and experiment on their own.
- All equipment should be clean and in good condition. It should be stored where it is visible to the children, and could be classified according to the type of activity planned. There should be enough equipment provided so that all the children at the tray can participate.
- Children should be encouraged to wash their hands after playing with sand.
- Children should be involved in clearing away and sweeping up at the end of the session.

Activity

You are responsible for planning an activity with sand for four-year-old children.

- Describe this activity and the equipment you would provide.
- How would this benefit their all-round development?

Clay

Like sand, clay is not usually played with at home. It is messy and needs the adult to have a relaxed attitude to the amount of mess it can make; otherwise some of the value of the material is lost. Children enjoy venting their aggression on clay, and it is particularly suitable for children who are upset or angry as it can be destroyed without incurring adult disapproval. Clay can be handled harshly, bashed about and will always resume its original form. It can be used very wet, and is then soothing and enjoyable.

Children proceed through different stages in their use of clay. At first they explore and experiment, then they repeat their experiments and practise handling the material and this leads on to more controlled use. From the age of about four, children may use clay as a modelling material.

In most establishments, terracotta or grey clay is used. There are other types available, such as New Clay, which sets very hard and does not need firing.

Amount of space		Type of space		Type of play		Adult involvement	
Whole area		Outside	✔	Solitary	✔	Essential	✔
Half area		Inside	✔	Parallel	✔	Enriching	✔
Quarter area		Hard surface	✔	Small group	✔	Not always necessary	
Small area	✔	Carpeted		Large group		Can be intrusive	✔
		Table space	✔				

Essential materials

- Clay
- Water
- Protective clothing
- Storage bin
- Space for drying.

Additional equipment

- Modelling and cutting tools
- Rolling pins and wooden mallets
- Artefacts for printing in clay, such as natural materials: shells, pine cones, pebbles; and construction equipment such as Lego bricks, Sticklebricks, etc.
- Bowls of water with different sponges.

Links to the EYFS

Personal, social and emotional development

Clay is often played with in a small group. It encourages children to share equipment and ideas. Children should help in clearing up afterwards. Clay also develops a respect for other children's creations.

It allows children to vent their feelings, particularly those of anger and frustration. When wet it is particularly relaxing and therapeutic. There does not have to be an end product, so clay is a non-judgemental experience.

Communication, language and literacy

Using clay encourages a range of vocabulary, such as 'malleable', 'mould', etc. Children in a group will discuss what they are making and many conversations may take place. Making marks in clay supports early reading.

Problem solving, reasoning and numeracy

Many mathematical experiences can be offered to children, for example Piaget's conservation tests (see pages 151–3). Opportunities arise for joint planning and decision making when children are constructing large models with other children.

Knowledge and understanding of the world

Children may explore how clay is used by different cultures, for example in producing cooking and lighting equipment. There could be museum trips to see artefacts made of clay or a visit to a potter. It can link in with curriculum projects on buildings and houses. Children can observe changes that occur when water is added to dry clay.

Physical development

Clay strengthens arm and finger muscles and promotes manipulative skills.

Creative development

Clay is a natural material, which inspires creativity and encourages an appreciation of other children's work. Clay is a wonderfully tactile experience and promotes the exploration of texture and form.

✓ Good practice: role of the adult

- It is particularly important to keep clay in good condition, as it quickly becomes dry and unusable, but properly stored it can be reused for many years. Store it in a bin with a well-fitting lid. Before putting clay away in the bin, knead it into a round or square shape, and insert water in a hole made by the thumb. If the clay does dry out, immerse it in a bucket of water, allow it to soften and you may then remould it. Try to prevent different types of clay being mixed together. The coolest part of the room is the best place to keep the clay bin. Rigid containers can be used for small amounts of clay – this is far safer than using plastic bags.
- Clay should be available every day.
- Children may need encouragement to work with clay. It is a good idea for you to sit at the table with the children, manipulating the clay, showing enjoyment. Even if it is not possible to position an adult at the clay table all the time, close supervision is necessary as clay can become very messy indeed if too much water is added. This would not matter if you were using the clay outside. Children's clothing must be well protected, and hands washed after play. Inside, it is sensible to put newspapers on the floor.
- A bucket of soapy water with a cloth or two in it is a good idea, as some children get upset if their hands are covered in clay.
- When children are first introduced to clay, there should not be any tools or equipment offered, as these tend to get in the way of sensory experiences.
- Equipment offered to older children should be planned to link with the curriculum. All tools should be in good condition and easily accessible. Give children the opportunity occasionally to plan their own activities.
- Not all children are drawn to clay; therefore you will be seen as a role model whilst displaying enthusiasm for this material.
- Never make models for the children to copy, even if they beg you to. This would interfere with their own creativity, as they would take your model as setting the standard.

 ## Activity

Plan a class project for five year olds, using clay. In what ways would your project develop their creativity?

Mud

Once children are mobile, most of them find out about mud quite quickly, and should be allowed to play with it outside freely if suitably dressed and fully immunised. You will need to check that the garden is free from pesticides and that no earth has been soiled by animals. Establishments should enquire of parents as to whether their children are protected against tetanus. Mud is one of the most enjoyable of natural materials for young children and is free and readily available in every garden. Mud can be mixed with water to give enjoyable sensory experiences, and can be seen to dry out to revert to dry soil. Small animals found in the mud give interest and pleasure to children, who often need to be persuaded to return them to their natural habitat.

Many centres nowadays prefer to use a mixture of compost bought from garden centres, pebbles and gravels, as garden soil may be contaminated. This mixture can also be used inside in pre-schools that have no outside play area.

Plasticine

This useful manufactured material is good for developing manipulative skills and for making models with older children. It is much cleaner and less messy than other malleable materials and is often familiar to children from their play at home, but it is not nearly as versatile or as tactile as other malleable materials. It can get hard very easily and needs storing in a warm environment. The colours tend to get mixed together, becoming a uniform sludge and should therefore be changed frequently so that it remains attractive to children. Discoloured plasticine should no longer be used by the children for modelling, but is very useful in propping up 3D displays, and in floating and sinking experiments.

Dough

Dough can be made in many ways and presented to children in a range of colours, and the children will enjoy participating in the mixing. By adding other ingredients, apart from the essential flour and water, different kinds of elasticity can be achieved. Salt should always be added as a preservative, and it will also ensure that children do not eat it. Dough should appear attractive, have enough elasticity without sticking to surfaces or fingers, and should last for at least a week in a sealed plastic container, kept in a cool place. Playing with dough is a relaxing, soothing social activity and is one often chosen by children when settling in to a new environment. Conversations around the dough table often stimulate a shy child to take part, as the experience helps relaxation. It can also be used in role play, and when baked and painted can be used to make models of food, in the same way as clay.

Activity

- Investigate at home, experimenting with different dough recipes using various flours, ingredients and colours. Record the one you found most successful.
- Having experienced this yourself, you might like to involve the children at your establishment in predicting and experimenting with various recipes.

Wood

Wood can be used either in the form of sawdust, and experimented with in a similar way to dry sand, or as offcuts of wood on a woodwork bench. All offcuts will need sanding down before use, so as to prevent splinters and should never have been treated with a preservative. Using wood to make models is a suitable activity for the older children in the group, but necessitates the presence of an adult to supervise the use of potentially dangerous tools. Tools should be scaled down versions of adult tools, and not toy ones. There is no value in a plastic hammer or screwdriver. Children need to have careful and repeated explanations of the dangers of

woodwork tools. This is a useful activity to present outside as the noise from banging and hammering will be less intrusive.

 Activity

How would you link working with wood to the EYFS?

Essential points

Anti-discriminatory practice

- Natural and malleable materials are enjoyed by all age groups and are culture- and gender-free experiences.
- Natural materials can be linked to themes looking at how materials are used throughout the world.
- Boys as well as girls can be encouraged in washing dolls and dolls' clothes, using dolls and clothes from a wide range of ethnic groups.
- Water, wood and sand encourage all the children to use scientific equipment and tools, and to become interested in technology, and this should be reinforced by the staff team.
- Disabled children particularly benefit from play with these materials, as an end product is not required, and all the experiences are pleasurable and therapeutic, increasing self-esteem and confidence. These activities are adaptable and can be used by children in wheelchairs or played with on the floor.

Safety

- Dry sand is often a hazard and needs careful supervision and thus is generally unsuitable for under threes. The floor needs to be swept regularly. Children should not be allowed to throw sand as this can cause choking, painful irritation in the eyes and is difficult to remove from tightly curly hair. All outside sand pits must be covered when not in use.
- Be aware of allergies among the children. Some natural materials may affect the skin. Sawdust and the dust from dry clay can cause breathing problems in some children.
- All children playing with any volume of water need constant observation and supervision, as drowning can occur very quickly. If children are playing with ice outside, they also need to be closely supervised as ice is dangerous if thrown.
- The floor must be mopped frequently to prevent falls on a slippery surface.
- If plastic bags are used for storing clay, they must be too small to go over children's heads and should not be left around. ▶

- Proper tools should be used when at the woodwork bench, as toy tools do not work properly and cause frustration. Therefore the bench must be supervised at all times, the correct tools used for the job and instruction given in the right way to use the tools. These must be kept in good condition and stored carefully when not in use. The number of children at the bench needs to be limited so that the adult can be sure that mishaps will not take place.
- Children should be discouraged from eating any of the materials.

Partnership with parents

- Make parents aware that children's clothes may get messy or wet when at the nursery or school, and that all their clothes should be easy to wash. Getting messy is a great deal of fun!

- Although some natural materials might not be suitable to be played with at home, water is the exception, and bathtime is an ideal opportunity for children to develop skills in pouring water, measuring volume and capacity, observing floating and sinking, and understanding such concepts as absorption when sponges are used. A display of water tools that are in everyday use, such as yoghurt pots, pebbles, tea strainers, corks and so on might inspire parents.

Resources

Evans D. and Williams C., 1994, *Water and Floating*, Dorling Kindersley Ltd.

Evans J., 2004, *10-Minute Ideas for Early Years: Sand and water*, Scholastic Publications Ltd.

Evans J., 2001, *Water Play*, Belair Early Years.

Gibson R. and Tyler J., 1989, *Playdough*, You and Your Child Series, Usborne Publishing.

Morris J., 1997, *Water*, Themes for Early Years Series, Scholastic Publications Ltd.

Sand and Water, Clay and Dough, PPA Learn Through Play Series, PPA.

Snyder Kaltman G., 2009, *Hands-On Learning*, Corwin Press.

Stocks S., 2003, *Traditional Activities Around the Year*, Step Forward Publishing Ltd.

West S. and Cox A., 2001, *Sand and Water Play: simple creative activities for young children*, Gryphon House Inc.

Websites
www.groundsforplay.com
www.childforms.com
www.littledreamers.com
www.childfun.com

5 Cooking

From a very young age, children enjoy watching and helping adults prepare and cook food. Food is a primary need, and encouraging children to cook and prepare food at home, and later in a pre-school group, helps to develop a sensory pleasure in food, which is such an important element of life. Children learn about food hygiene and balanced meals, how to make choices in the supermarkets for taste and value, and where different foods come from.

It is possible today to buy food from all around the world, and by using recipes from other countries children learn about many cultures in a most enjoyable way. 'Cooking' covers a wide range of activities in the classroom, from making a sandwich to producing a complicated meal. Unlike most experiences introduced in the pre-school, cooking has an end product. It therefore follows that the adult has to be more involved and needs to direct the children to a certain extent. For this reason, it is even more important that the children do as much as possible for themselves, being involved from the preparation stage through to sharing the end product, and thought must be given as to which foods and recipes are suitable for group cooking.

Amount of space		Type of space		Type of play		Adult involvement	
Whole area		Outside		Solitary	✔	Essential	✔
Half area		Inside	✔	Parallel		Enriching	
Quarter area		Hard surface	✔	Small group	✔	Not always necessary	
Small area	✔	Carpeted		Large group			
		Table space	✔			Can be intrusive	

Essential materials
- Protective clothing, preferably used only for cooking
- Floor mop
- Range of good quality cooking utensils, such as bowls, plates, forks, knives, spoons of various sizes, baking trays, saucepans
- Hot water, for clearing up afterwards
- Recipes and ingredients.

Suggested additional equipment
- Kettle
- Access to an oven or microwave, and to a fridge

- Oven gloves for adult
- Scales
- A rotary whisk
- A sieve
- Palette knife.

Links to the EYFS

Personal, social and emotional development

When children work cooperatively in a group, they share utensils, equipment and food, take turns, develop awareness of different eating patterns and cultural diversity and learn the need to clear away efficiently. Safety rules have to be learnt and followed.

Cooking gives independence through the ability to cook for oneself. Cooking promotes pride and self-esteem and, although not all children wish to eat what they have cooked, the activity nevertheless produces a valued end product. It is an enjoyable reminder of home. Tension is released when beating, kneading and whipping food.

Communication, language and literacy

Children will have to listen carefully in order to gain new vocabulary, such as 'dissolving' and 'freezing', and 'liquid' and 'solid'. They will also learn correct mathematical and scientific terms, express their needs, ask questions and consult with adults. Recipes and labelling make links with reading and writing, as does the recognition of different scripts if the food is labelled in a different language. Listening to and following instructions aids concentration.

Problem solving, reasoning and numeracy

By helping to plan the activity, children gain shopping skills such as making lists, choosing ingredients and handling money. Cooking enforces a range of mathematical and scientific concepts, such as weighing, measuring, recognition of number, volume, expansion and contraction, fractions, sequencing, patterns, density, temperature, etc.

Knowledge and understanding of the world

Knowledge of foods from many cultures will be gained, and they will understand which tools are appropriate for each recipe, and how food changes due to temperature change or combining. They will see how to use gas and electricity safely. They will begin to understand basic nutrition and healthy eating patterns. Cooking promotes an understanding of nutritional principles, home safety and hygiene.

Children from the age of six will begin to follow recipes from a book.

Physical development

Cooking develops large muscles in the arms when pouring, rolling, kneading, stirring, mixing and whisking, and in lifting trays, bowls and tins. It involves fine and gross manipulative skills, such as measuring, spooning liquids and solids, cracking eggs, decorating buns, cutting up fruit and vegetables, making sandwiches.

Creative development

Children enjoy the apparent 'magical' changes due to food combinations and temperature. They learn about the attractive presentation of food and of links between food and religious and cultural festivals. Food can be an overwhelming sensory experience involving taste, smell, touch, sight and sounds.

Activity

Start to compile a book of recipes that you have used with the children.

- How could you involve the children in making this book?
- How would you evaluate the making of these recipes to the children's development and learning?
- Which of the recipes that you have used so far has allowed the children to participate the most?

Good practice: role of the adult

- Careful planning and preparation is necessary, thought being given to age-appropriate experiences.
- All food must be very fresh and in excellent condition, and dried goods stored in airtight containers. Utensils must be scrupulously clean, and table tops wiped with hot soapy water and a clean cloth before use. Hands need to be washed, and nails scrubbed. Long hair should be tied back. Children with colds, sores or cuts should be excluded from the activity until they are well.
- Aprons should be used just for cooking. It is useful to have a clean cloth and a bowl of hot soapy water available in case of spills.
- A range of cooking activities should be offered to the children, from simple jelly making, which shows how heat changes food, to more complicated

recipes that require mixing several ingredients. Remember to cook savoury as well as sweet foods. Proper cooking techniques, such as slicing and whipping, should be demonstrated.

- All cooking activities have value, but the most important thing for the children is to be involved in every aspect of the experience, if possible from discussing what they are about to cook, to shopping for the ingredients, preparing the equipment, producing the food, washing and clearing up, and relating what they have achieved to the rest of the class, who should also take part in the eating. Enough food should be cooked so that the whole group can enjoy the end product.
- The activity should be organised so that children do not have to handle very hot liquids, and only the adult uses the oven.
- Nearly all children enjoy cooking, so you must make sure that it takes place often, and that all children have a turn. To ensure that children get the most from the experience, four is the maximum number, and this can be achieved by having only four cooking aprons, and adhering strictly to a rota system. Try to avoid always cooking sweet food, as cooking at school or in nursery is an opportunity for children to try out new tastes and develop a more sophisticated palate. The constant presence of an adult is needed, for safety and hygiene reasons, to answer and ask questions, to foster language development, to encourage manipulative skills and to ensure fair turn-taking.

Activity

Plan a party for a group of five year olds where the children are involved in the planning and preparation of the food.

Essential points

Anti-discriminatory practice

- Cooking is an experience enjoyed equally by boys and girls and presents an opportunity for them to work together. Avoid making stereotypical assumptions about gender and racial preferences.
- When deciding on a cooking activity, check that no child is prevented from participating due to cultural or religious diet prohibitions.
- The sharing of food experiences and different utensils from around the world shifts children away from a narrow perception of food preparation. It offers many opportunities for making traditional dishes and linking in with cultural and religious festivals. ▶

- Cooking is especially valuable for children who have special needs or learning disabilities as it encourages independence and self-reliance. Care must be taken to ensure that no child is allergic to anything you wish to cook or that it contravenes a special diet.

Safety

- Close supervision is essential at all times. Preparation must be very thorough, and it is important to have all the necessary equipment and ingredients to hand so as not to leave the children unattended. Cooker guards must be used if the oven is in the same room as the children and they need to be taught about the dangers of heat, and how to handle sharp knives safely. An adult should always put food in and out of the oven, and the rules of safety should be frequently stated and observed through good role modelling.
- No wires should be allowed to trail on the floor.
- Any spills on the floor should be mopped up immediately to avoid accidents.
- A first aid box should be nearby in case of cuts or burns.
- A fire extinguisher and a fire blanket must be kept near the oven.
- Potentially dangerous items of equipment should be stored out of the way of children, and put away immediately after use.

Partnership with parents

- Cooking is an everyday activity in the home and so provides a perfect home–school link. Parents are a useful resource for information concerning food preparation and recipes.

- Some parents might like to cook with a small group of children from time to time, and could bring in recipes and ingredients that might be new to some children. From recipe books made by the children in school, parents might like to try out their children's ideas. Displays showing healthy eating choices could be shared with parents. Encourage parents to allow children to be involved in making their food.

Activity

Describe two cooking experiences, one for 2–3 year olds, and one for 4–5 year olds, and say why these are particularly appropriate for the age groups.

Resources

Braman A., 2000, *Kids Around the World Cook! The best food and recipes from many lands*, John Wiley.

Cook D., 2008, *The Kids' Multicultural Cookbook: Food and Fun Around the World*, Ideals Publishing.

De Boo M., 1990, *Science Activities*, Bright Ideas for Early Years Series, Scholastic Publications Ltd.

Drew H., 2006, *First Baking Activity Book*, Dorling Kindersley.

Dunbar K., 1992, *The Spice of Life*, Belair.

Lynn S. and James D., 1999, *Fun Food: I Can Make It*, Two-Can Publishing Ltd.

Robins D., 1998, *Kids' Round-the-world Cookbook*, New edition, Kingfisher Books.

Whiting M. and Lobstein T., 1998, *The Nursery Food Book*, 2nd edition, Hodder Arnold.

Wilkes A., 2003, *The Children's Step-by-step Cook Book*, Dorling Kindersley.

Young C., 2000, *Round the World Cookbook*, Usborne Publishing.

Websites

www.foodforlifeuk.org

www.organix.com

www.healthykids.org.uk

6 Imaginary Play

Imaginary play grows out of imitative play. Babies from a very early age imitate adults in games of 'Peek-a-boo', waving goodbye and copying actions. Later, children do not need a direct role model in front of them, but will start to use their memory, pouring out imaginary cups of tea for all and sundry, and pretending to eat non-existent food.

At around two years, children start to take on roles. One will be the 'mummy', and another the 'daddy', and this will gradually extend to include the baby, the big sister and even a visiting aunt. As children become older, role play will be extended to other people who are familiar in their lives or from books and television. The provision of dressing-up clothes often stimulates the imagination of the children. It is best to provide clothes that can be used in many different ways, the only exception being those used in the hospital corner, where children need a more realistic environment to allay their fears.

In the pre-school environment, domestic play, such as family roles, mealtimes, bedtimes and so on, is carried out in the role play corner. This activity gives a great deal of comfort to the young child, particularly those starting school or nursery.

In 2003, Penny Holland, a lecturer in Early Childhood Studies at the University of North London, carried out a small study in an under fives centre where boys were allowed to develop their interest in bouts of gun play (not involving the use of manufactured toy guns). This seemed to suggest that boys gained the confidence to move on to more imaginative play, including dressing up. In correspondence with Anne Longfield, the director of the Kids Club Network, Penny Holland suggests that the zero tolerance approach to gun play does not work. She feels that being negative about such play leads to lack of self-esteem, stunted imaginative development and turns them into creative liars, and that being allowed to play symbolically in this way will let them flourish imaginatively and emotionally, and that in time there will be less aggressive play. On the other hand, Anne Longfield can see no place for any type of gun play in pre-schools as this weakens the message that guns and violence are unacceptable.

Although discouraged in most homes and pre-school establishments, and to the despair of many parents and teachers, children do have imaginary shoot-outs, but they do not need toy guns, since Lego bricks will do just as well. But it is from this ability to **symbolise** inanimate objects that the readiness for reading grows, as a child starts to understand that those inky blobs on a page stand for real words in a story.

Within your group, discuss your placement's attitude to gun play.

For some children, acting out a role can be a release of emotions through pretending to be someone else. A child who is constantly listening to adults quarrelling may find it helpful to pretend to be one of those adults, and have some say of their own. This type of play can give you an insight into possible difficulties at home, but caution must be exercised, as the children could be acting out what they have seen on the television the night before. On the other hand, never disregard what a child might be trying to tell you, until it has been completely checked out and discussed with your supervisor. Observations will come in very useful here, as this will give you an opportunity of discussing the child with your supervisor, who may have more knowledge of the child's background.

A child waiting to go into hospital will find it very useful to be a make-believe patient, as a way of expressing emotions and fears.

Some children, who may be withdrawn or shy, may still have difficulty in expressing their emotions. Puppets can be a great help here, as the child uses them to voice hidden feelings. Ready-made puppets should be introduced cautiously, as small children can be fearful of a toy that seems to have a life of its own. It might be

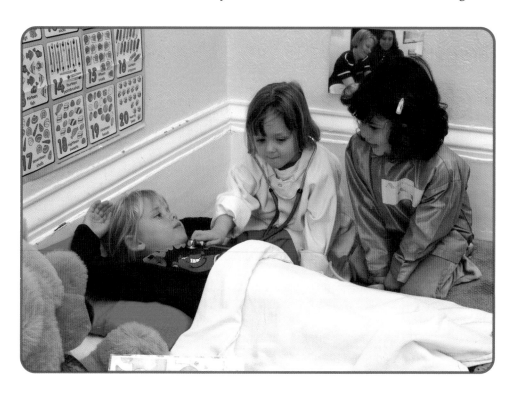

far better to get the children to make their own puppets, even if they are only made from a cereal box or a paper bag.

As children are small, vulnerable people, they enjoy acting out roles of super-heroes. This makes them feel empowered and strong, and is a boost to their self-esteem.

Children play with dolls in different ways at each stage of their development. Once babies start to walk, they will use the doll as any other inanimate object, just holding onto it anywhere (usually the feet) and dragging it after them. At about two years, some children will start to cuddle the doll, treating it more as a baby, particularly if there has been a recent birth in the family. This doll might come in for some very hard knocks! A little later on, children enjoy bathing dolls, dressing (but mainly undressing) dolls and taking them out for walks in a push-chair. At about six years, groups of children might play with several dolls, having pretend tea parties or schoolrooms. Many girls and boys start to collect dolls, such as Barbie and Action Man, and there is often rivalry in the collecting of their clothes and artefacts.

Small-scale models of people, animals, vehicles, dolls houses and items of domestic equipment are often used in imaginary play. They are familiar to the children, and the play allows them to relax, and extend and develop language. These toys can be used in conjunction with other equipment in the nursery or school classroom, such as the sand tray and the role play corner.

For some imaginary activities, it is best to use the real equipment; for example, when setting up a hairdresser's salon, a dentist's surgery or a hospital ward, the proper tools of the trade are readily available, and add more to the play. You obviously do not provide the more dangerous equipment!

You will become aware that more imaginary play takes place when there are fewer directed activities. With the permission of your supervisor, you might like to try the experiment of providing nothing for the children for the first half hour or so, and note how the children are able to amuse themselves, mainly in imaginary play.

Amount of space		Type of space		Type of play		Adult involvement	
Whole area		Outside	✔	Solitary	✔	Essential	
Half area	✔	Inside	✔	Parallel	✔	Enriching	✔
Quarter area	✔	Hard surface	✔	Small group	✔	Not always necessary	✔
Small area	✔	Carpeted	✔	Large group	✔	Can be intrusive	✔
		Table space	✔				

Essential materials

- None.

Suggested additional materials

- Role play corner and domestic play equipment
- Small world toys
- Dressing-up clothes, particularly hats, wigs and pieces of material and clothing worn by different cultural groups, such as saris, shalwar kameez and Chinese slippers
- Jewellery
- Keys
- Dolls and dolls clothes
- Puppets
- Empty cardboard boxes, tubes and cartons
- Wooden blocks
- Specialist equipment, linked to certain professions, such as a vet's corner, or a health clinic.

Links to the EYFS

Personal, social and emotional development

Imaginary play allows children to experience the roles of others. Children often play together in large and small groups, as some imaginary games need social interaction. Children have to take turns and share equipment. Imaginary play allows children to display caring and social skills, e.g. nursing, parenting and showing hospitality, and encourages children to explore different cultural backgrounds in the use of multicultural domestic equipment and clothes. Children start to form their own identity through role/imaginary play. This type of play also allows children to express and release positive and negative emotions. It gives confidence, and allows self-esteem to develop. Playing roles empowers children, and lets them glimpse and begin to come to terms with the adult world. Domestic play is a link with home, and very comforting to the insecure child, or a child experiencing a new situation. Playing with dolls can allow a child to express negative feelings, without harm to a new addition to the family.

Communication, language and literacy

Imaginary play stimulates language and the use of new vocabulary, particularly with the involvement of a sympathetic and sensitive adult. It promotes discussion on life experiences. Doll play can lead on to discussion about reproduction and childcare. Imaginary play presents opportunities for children to direct and organise activities, promotes creativity and may lead to writing imaginative stories. Symbolising everyday objects leads to an understanding of print.

Problem solving, reasoning and numeracy

Domestic play offers mathematical experiences in matching and sorting and **one-to-one correspondence**, by laying tables and putting crockery and cutlery away in the correct place. Graded dolls and dolls' clothes help children understand concepts of small, medium and large, and can give children a range of mathematical experiences.

Knowledge and understanding of the world

Imaginary play presents opportunities to participate in other cultures, and encourages an appreciation of other children's life experiences.

Physical development

Imaginary play can be very energetic, particularly when enacting superheroes. Large muscles are used when dressing up. Manipulative skills and hand–eye coordination are used in fastening clothes, dressing dolls, handling domestic equipment and in playing with small world toys.

Creative development

Rich materials give tactile experiences, for example in handling clothing and fabrics. Imaginary play aids problem-solving by encouraging a child to invent new ways of doing things. Using objects in imaginative ways, not necessarily for the function for which they were designed, helps children to have fun and indulge in fantasy, with no expected end result.

✓ Good practice: role of the adult

- Imaginary play is sometimes undervalued, but time, space and opportunity should be provided every day. Constant observation will ensure that you facilitate and extend such opportunities.
- All equipment should be kept in good order, and children can help with this. Clothes should be hung on hangers, cleaned and repaired routinely, and removed once this is no longer possible. There should be enough dressing-up materials to allow different themes to be acted out, and for every child to have access to something. Clothing from all cultures should be treated with respect, and the adult team should be knowledgeable in the correct naming and wearing of clothing, such as saris and turbans. Some imaginary play can be repetitious, such as that based on television characters. The intervention of an adult can often add a new dimension to the play.

- The role of the adult is a sensitive one in imaginative play. This play should be encouraged but remember that children need their privacy, and the opportunity to develop the play in their own way. Adults should wait to be invited, and should then see themselves as an equal participant, not a dominant one. Sensitively adding new vocabulary to the conversation aids language development. By knowing that children might be facing a particular difficulty, such as the birth of a new baby or perhaps hospital admission, you can help by setting up an environment in which babies can be cared for, or hospital procedures carried out. Fear of the dentist or the barber can be allayed by make-believe play in the 'surgery' or the 'hairdresser'.

Essential points

Anti-discriminatory practice

- You may see children using stereotypes in their role play, copying situations observed in their environment. You will have to challenge this behaviour in a sensitive way. Imaginary play allows boys to take on and dress up in perceived female roles such as the mother or the ballerina, whilst girls can be fathers and fire-fighters. Sometimes boys need to be encouraged to use the role play corner, as this may be seen as the girls' domain.
- Equipment, clothes and pretend food from many cultures should be provided in the role play corner. Dolls and small world people should also reflect the multicultural world, with different skin tones and ethnic features.
- Children in wheelchairs should have access to the role play corner.
- Children challenged in any special way need as much or more opportunity for imaginary play. This might necessitate more involvement on the part of the staff.
- Make sure the neck openings of dressing-up clothes are wide and that trousers are wide enough to fit over callipers. Some of your resources should reflect disability, such as puppets with hearing aids, or dolls in wheelchairs.

Safety

- Children enjoy wearing adult shoes, particularly high heels, as this not only gives them height, but also a feeling of importance. They should never be allowed to wear such shoes outside, or with any climbing equipment. Clothes that are too long are a similar hazard. Clothing such as scarves, ties and belts draped around the neck is obviously dangerous. Some jewellery might have sharp pins or clasps, and bead necklaces can break and be swallowed.

▶

A Practical Guide to Activities for Young Children

When real equipment is used in make-believe play, such as the dentist's surgery, you will obviously provide only safe equipment, such as dental mirrors, toothbrushes and toothpaste. Electrical equipment, such as hairdryers or food mixers, needs to have plugs and wires removed before being used in play. The use of water needs to be monitored. All equipment must be checked regularly.

Activities

- Observe children aged two years and four years playing with dolls. How does their behaviour differ?
- Make a cloak from a piece of material gathered at one end with elastic. Do the boys and girls play with it in the same way?
- Try to identify the different types of imaginary play that occur in the nursery/classroom. How much is spontaneous? How much is adult-directed?
- Add an item to the home area to extend imaginative play. Observe the outcome.

Partnership with parents

- Parents and friends could be encouraged to lend or give clothing, so that there is always some in reserve. Be aware, however, that some parents may lend something of sentimental value, so always check with parents that they understand the object may be damaged in the play.
- On occasion, parents might feel anxious if their child is taking on a role of which they disapprove. Try to involve parents in the play, and explain how valuable such play can be.

Resources

Beckles Wilson R. and Gray L., 1993, *Just Imagine*, Blair.

Caudron C., Childs C. and Gibson L., 1995, *Dressing Up*, How To Make Series, Usborne Publishing.

Duffy B., 2006, *Supporting Creativity and Imagination in the Early Years*, 2nd edition, OUP.

Garnett S., 1996, *Home Corner*, Learning Through Play Series, Scholastic Publications Ltd.

Heald C. and McNicholas S., 2002, *Role Play Activities*, Scholastic Publications Ltd.

Hobart C., Frankel J. and Walker M. (Series Editor), 2009, *A Practical Guide to Child Observation and Assessment*, 4th edition, Nelson Thornes.

Holland P., 2003, *We Don't Play with Guns Here*, OUP.

Leach B., 1997, *Small World Play*, Learning Through Play Series, Scholastic Publications Ltd.

Websites

www.bigeyedowl.co.uk/roleplay.htm

www.kidsource.com

Equipment

Galt supplies the Dara Doll and a set of callipers, crutches, spectacles and hearing aids. Galt, Sovereign House, Stockport Road, Cheadle, Cheshire SK8 2EA. Telephone: 0161 428 8511.

J. and M. Toys are specialists in dressing-up clothes, including clothes from around the world. J. and M. Toys, 46 Finsbury Drive, Wrose, Bradford, W. Yorks BD2 1QA. Telephone: 01274 599 314.

7 Painting and Drawing

This chapter covers spontaneous painting and drawing, carried out by young children, undirected by adults.

All children should be offered frequent opportunities to paint and draw when they feel inclined. When very young, before fluent speech, spontaneous painting and drawing is a most valuable means of expression. The benefit of children being able to express themselves in this way is reduced if adults insist on questioning children about their paintings, suggesting additions to the work and wanting titles for every painting or drawing.

Adults interpreting children's paintings are quite often wrong. Children love to do all-dark, one-colour paintings at some stage in their development – this does not mean that something terrible has happened to them that they wish to forget! Understanding what stage of development children might have reached through interpreting their paintings is interesting, and there are many books on this subject.

Amount of space		Type of space		Type of play		Adult involvement	
Whole area		Outside	✔	Solitary	✔	Essential	
Half area		Inside	✔	Parallel	✔	Enriching	
Quarter area	✔	Hard surface	✔	Small group		Not always necessary	
Small area	✔	Carpeted		Large group		Can be intrusive	✔
		Table space	✔				

Essential materials

For painting:

- Protection for clothing
- Old newspapers for protecting the floor, the easel and the table top
- A floor mop
- Facilities for drying paintings
- Paints, paper, brushes, clean water.

For drawing:

- Pencils and paper
- Chubby crayons for the youngest children.

Suggested additional equipment

For painting:

- Large variety of paints and brushes
- Various thicknesses of paint
- Various materials, such as sand, to change the texture of the paint
- Various sizes, textures, shapes and colours of paper
- Non-spillable paint containers
- Pots to mix colours in
- A drying rack or line.

For drawing:

- Crayons, felt pens, pastels, chalks and charcoal
- Chalkboards
- Various sizes, textures, shapes and colours of paper.

Links to the EYFS

Personal, social and emotional development

Spontaneous painting is not generally a social activity, although sometimes you may see two children painting side by side, discussing what they are painting with each other, and perhaps sharing their experiences and feelings.

Painting, in particular, often allows children to express emotions that they find difficult to put into words. It is an enjoyable new activity for many young children on starting nursery. Attaining this skill leads to a sense of achievement and self-esteem.

Communication, language and literacy

This is not an experience that particularly develops language, but the child might want to discuss the painting or drawing with an adult or another child. Symbolic blobs lead to the foundation of reading and writing.

Problem solving, reasoning and numeracy

Painting and drawing lend themselves to pattern creation. The exploration of materials, textures and techniques expands knowledge of colour and shapes. It helps children to understand spatial relationships and composition.

Knowledge and understanding of the world

Painting allows children to experiment with a variety of materials, and observe the change in the materials, particularly when helping to mix the powder paints.

Physical development

Painting at the easel develops large muscles in the arms of the younger child. As the child gains more control, finer manipulative skills are developed, aiding hand–eye coordination. Development of sight and touch are promoted by painting and drawing.

Creative development

Painting and drawing develop an aesthetic awareness of composition, colour, shape, patterns and relationships. They encourage imagination and creativity.

Activity

Visit an art gallery in your area.

- What category of painting did you enjoy most?
- Were there any artists you disliked? If so, why?
- Did the gallery have an educational department?
- Would the children in your placement enjoy a visit there? What paintings, in particular, would you like them to see, and how could you use the visit in your practice?

Good practice: role of the adult

- Painting is a messy activity, which is why it is not always done at home, and therefore young children should be given every opportunity to explore this medium undisturbed whenever they wish.
- Aprons in good condition should be provided.
- Tables, easels and the floor should be covered in newspaper and cleaned regularly. A mop and bucket should be placed nearby and the children should have easy access to the bathroom.
- The children will get the most from painting and drawing if they are left to pursue it on their own. Adults should not interrupt, ask questions about the picture or make suggestions. They should never paint or draw for the child, or impose their ideas and concepts. Children will think the adult interpretation is the superior one, and this will discourage them from valuing their own work and may stunt their creativity. Outline or character shapes should never be provided for the children.
- The use of templates and colouring-in books is not good practice as it limits creativity.
- The activity should be presented attractively, and sited where the light is good. Paints should be of a creamy consistency and mixed freshly every day. The children might want to help with this. There should be a good range of colours, and each paint pot should have its own brush so as to keep the colours clear and bright. All drawing materials should be in good condition, and there should be enough provided.
- There should be a choice of paper, placed so that the children can help themselves. A drying area for paintings is a necessity.
- It is obtrusive to some children to put their names on their paintings and drawings. Always ask the child first. Children usually do not want to take their work home; once they have done the activity it has no more interest for them. Nursery staff who insist on paintings and drawings going home risk the children's disappointment if the parent does not value the work sufficiently.
- Only add a title or comments if the child asks you to, and use the child's words.
- Drawing is not always a solitary activity, and friends often sit at a table and draw together. Children's drawings show developmental stages more clearly than paintings and are most useful to keep for recording purposes.
- A visit to an art gallery can be useful in generating interest and discussion.

- Make a book of paintings and drawings by the children in the nursery or school, adding their ages, and showing clearly the different stages of development that the children have reached.

- If you were asked to paint or draw a picture without being given a theme or title, would you be able to do this? Identify any areas of difficulty. Why do you think children can do it so naturally?

Essential points

Anti-discriminatory practice

- Painting and drawing are essentially culture-free and gender-free activities. Make sure that the range of colours allows children from all ethnic groups to represent themselves and their families realistically, should they want to do so.
- The National Curriculum dictates that children should develop an awareness of art from a young age. Care must be taken to show children the work of a wide range of artists, and not just that of European males.
- Children with disabilities will enjoy and learn a great deal from using painting and drawing materials. All children have access to this experience. Standing frames can be used for motor-impaired children, to support them while painting.
- Visually-impaired children would benefit from tactile and fluorescent materials, and textured paper. Short, stubby brushes are easier to handle.

Safety

- Very young children need watching to make sure they do not eat the paint. All paint used must be lead-free and non-toxic.
- Children should be discouraged from walking around with pencils or brushes in their mouths, or from chewing lead pencils.
- Remove pen tops when being used by very young children, to avoid the possibility of choking.
- Major spills should be mopped up quickly to avoid the possibility of falls.
- Hand washing after painting should be supervised.

Partnership with parents

- For the child, the process of painting is important, and parents should be told that some children do not even recognise a painting they have done as the finished product is not important to them, but if parents are offered a painting to take home, they should be encouraged to welcome the offering and treat it with respect.

- As painting is an integral part of the curriculum, make parents aware that clothes may get messy, and that children should only wear clothes that can be washed easily.

- Display and update details of local art exhibitions regularly.

Resources

Ali Eglington K., 2003, *Art in the Early Years*, RoutledgeFalmer.

Cox M., 1992, *Children's Drawings*, Penguin.

De Boo M., 1995, *Colour*, Themes for Early Years Series, Scholastic Publications Ltd.

FitzMaurice Mills J., 1991, *Art for Our Children*, Wolfhound Press.

Gardner H., 1982, *Artful Scribbles*, New edition, Basic Books.

Gibson R. and Barlow A., 2002, *What Shall I Draw?*, Usborne Publishing.

Kellogg R., 1969, *Analysing Children's Art*, Mayfield Publishing Co.

Matthews J., 1994, *Helping Children to Draw and Paint in Early Childhood*, Hodder & Stoughton.

Williams D., 1997, *Step by Step Art for Nursery/Reception Classes*, Topical Resources.

Wolfe G., 1997, *The Children's Art Book*, Bellew Publishing.

Websites

www.ednoland.com

www.artforschools.com

www.nationalgallery.org.uk

www.npg.org.uk

www.tate.org.uk

www.art-works.org.uk

Educational visits

The Tate Galleries will organise free nursery workshops. Telephone the education department to book: 020 7887 8888.

8 Creative Art Activities

Under this heading we have grouped all activities that involve creative thought on the part of the child, but are generally adult directed. For example, the modelling of **recyclable materials** is dependent on the materials provided by the adult, and printing is directed by the way the adult sets up the activity.

If children are allowed to use their own ideas within the constraints named above, creative art activities will stimulate their imagination and aesthetic awareness, encourage their creativity, aid social development by sharing materials and turn-taking, learning about the properties of various materials, and developing language skills as the children have to understand instructions and ask questions. Many activities will link in with the curriculum.

Children usually work in small groups with an adult supervising, and sometimes the whole class is involved as part of a theme that is being explored.

Suggested activities

The following list of suggestions for creative art activities is not comprehensive.

Printing

Activities could include printing with vegetables, fruits, sponges, Lego bricks, Sticklebricks, leaves and string using paints, inks and dyes. Hand and foot prints and toy cars can also be used.

Recyclable material modelling

All shapes and sizes of cartons, containers, pots and odds and ends can be employed, using various types of glue, paste, Blu-Tack™ and sticky tape.

Painting

Painting ideas include butterfly prints, drip paintings, paintings in different shades of one colour, marble painting, oil painting, sugar painting, bubble painting, straw painting and making patterns.

Older children may be encouraged to draw objects, plants or animals in a realistic way.

Collage

Use paper of all kinds, such as tissue, sweet papers, postcards, magazine pictures and foil; other manufactured materials such as polystyrene chips, pieces of fabric, bottle tops and straws; and natural materials such as leaves, sand, twigs, seeds, shells, bark, wood and shavings.

Pasta and pulses can be used, but as with printing with food, some establishments might feel this is not ethically correct.

Messy play

Some activities provided for children are not adult directed in the same way. Messy play, such as playing with cooked spaghetti mixed with liquid detergent and colouring, or experimenting with cornflour and water, is enjoyable for all children, but particularly so for the youngest ones. A large sheet of paper can be attached to the wall, and paint in squeezy bottles can be squirted at it. Finger painting comes into this category; paints and paste are mixed together, and patterns made in the mixture with the fingers. Older children might like to print their creations.

 Activity

Make a list of the creative art activities that take place often in your establishment.

- Which ones most extend children's all-round development?
- Are there any that you feel are not very useful?

Essential materials

- Protection for clothing, the table top and the floor; floor mop and sponge for table spills
- Facilities for drying work
- Basin of water and towel to hand, to remove surplus materials.

Other materials depend on chosen activity.

Amount of space		Type of space		Type of play		Adult involvement	
Whole area		Outside	✔	Solitary	✔	Essential	✔
Half area		Inside	✔	Parallel	✔	Enriching	
Quarter area		Hard surface	✔	Small group	✔	Not always necessary	
Small area	✔	Carpeted		Large group			
		Table space	✔			Can be intrusive	

Links to the EYFS

Personal, social and emotional development

Creative art activities help children learn to share and take turns to work cooperatively on a group project, and to understand the rules of working in a group.

It provides enjoyment, a sense of achievement, independence, autonomy and self-esteem. A sense of purpose is developed in older children in producing a piece of finished work.

Communication, language and literacy

New vocabulary is learnt, particularly positional language such as 'under' and 'over'. Understanding instructions and asking questions develops comprehension and expressive speech. Printing encourages symbol recognition through mark making.

Problem solving, reasoning and numeracy

Many mathematic and scientific concepts may be explored. Patterns may lead to understanding of **spatial relationships**. Children learn to measure and explore space and shape. This is one of the best activities for intellectual development, as children use their imagination and creativity in planning and producing this work. Children's concentration span is often extended in a well thought out, enjoyable activity.

Knowledge and understanding of the world

Different materials encourage exploration and experimentation and this, in turn, leads to an understanding of design and technology, and encourages the effective and skilful use of tools. The different properties of the materials are explored and experienced. Creative art activities link in well with festivals and celebrations.

Physical development

Creative art activities help children to develop arm muscles and fine manipulative skills leading to hand–eye coordination. Many of the materials and textures used will encourage tactile development, and colours will stimulate vision.

Creative development

These activities stimulate aesthetic awareness and the beginning of art appreciation, in pattern making, composition, use of colour and attractive materials.

✔ Good practice: role of the adult

Most of the points made about the role of the adult in Chapter 7 Painting and Drawing remain true for creative art activities, with some additions, as follows.

- You should always prepare enough materials for all the children who wish to participate. This might not be possible during one session, but you can always repeat the activity later in the week.
- Some children may prefer not to be involved, and this should be respected.
- It becomes important for children to produce finished work as they progress through infant school, but children under the age of five should be allowed just to explore the possibilities of the materials and take part at that level. If the expectation always to finish a creative art activity is stressed too much, some children might find taking part a negative experience.
- Although essentially adult directed, children can still be involved in choosing a creative activity, and these should be available at most sessions.
- Make sure all materials are kept in good order, especially those filling the scrap box. Throw out materials that become torn or damaged. Discourage the use of insides of lavatory rolls, as these are not hygienic.
- Before embarking on any creative art experience, make sure that it will be valuable to the children. Some activities, such as filling in an outline of a snowman with scrunched-up pieces of white tissue paper, are of little value, and children take limited satisfaction in carrying out such useless tasks. Why not get them to help you wash the paint pots and the aprons instead: they will learn a great deal more from this than colouring in templates!

Activity

Plan a walk in the local park with the children. List items you might collect that could be used in a collage.

Essential points

Anti-discriminatory practice

See Chapter 7 Painting and Drawing, and also the following points.

- Blowing paint through a straw to make pictures develops mouth muscles and can help poor speech expression.
- Children with visual impairment should be encouraged to participate, using many different materials. They should not be forbidden the use of any tools, and they will need to be instructed in their correct use. They may need to work at an unusual angle.

Safety

- If very young children are involved or near the activity area, ensure they do not eat any of the materials, or insert any small objects into noses or ears.
- Before beginning bubble painting, ask the child to blow through the straw on to your hand first so that she does not swallow the paint and detergent by mistake.
- All materials that could be dangerous, such as scissors, need close supervision.
- Red kidney beans are poisonous when raw and should not be used in collage.
- Pen tops should be removed before use as they can be inhaled if put in the mouth and the child might choke.
- Anti-fungicide paste should never be used as it is very toxic.
- Polystyrene trays should be washed before use as they may be contaminated with bacteria.
- Not all materials are suitable. Cigarette packets, bleach bottles, egg boxes and toilet roll tubes should never be used.
- Be alert to any child with allergies. For example, a child with a nut allergy could be at risk from a cereal box that once contained nuts.
- Superglue should never be used, for obvious reasons.

Partnership with parents

- Parents may be asked to bring in materials, and you will need to make sure these are appropriate. A list of wanted materials might be put up on the parents' notice board.
- Many parents will be artistic and might like to share their skills in the nursery or classroom.
- If the work is well displayed, parents might ask questions as to how to carry out the activity at home.
- Parents sometimes show concern that messy activities will spoil their children's clothes. Stains are more easily removed if a little washing up liquid is added to the paint.

Activity

Plan a creative art activity with five-year-old children. List the values of this activity to the areas of development.

Resources

Burgess L., 1994, *Art Activities*, Bright Ideas for Early Years Series, Scholastic Publications Ltd.

Chambers J. and Hood M., 1990, *Simply Artistic*, Belair Publications.

Deshpande C., 1994, *Celebrations*, World Wide Crafts Series, A.&C. Black (Publishers) Ltd.

Einon D., 2005, *Creative Play for 2–5s*, Hamlyn.

Gadd T. and Morton D., 1992, *Technology Key Stage 1*, Blueprint Series, Nelson Thornes Ltd.

Gibson R., 2002, *What Shall I Paint?*, Usborne Publishing.

Gibson R. and Tyler J., 1990, *Paper Play*, You and Your Child Series, Usborne Publishing.

Gulliver A. and Turnbull S., 2003, *Things to Make and Do with Paper*, Usborne Publishing.

Leach B., 1997, *Junk Materials*, Learning Through Play Series, Scholastic.

Perkins S., 1998, *Seeing, Making, Doing: creative development in Early Years settings*, National Early Years Network.

Sharman L., 1994, *Amazing Book of Shapes*, Dorling Kindersley Ltd.

Wolfe G., 1997, *The Children's Activity Book*, Bellew Publishing.

Websites
www.dltk-kids.com
www.underfives.co.uk
www.crayola.com
www.kidsdomain.com

9 Small and Large Construction

Most children will have some construction sets at home. Even babies enjoy building towers and knocking them down. The establishment will have a greater variety of bricks and blocks, and also more space to accommodate large buildings.

Blocks

A bag of bricks is the most versatile piece of equipment that any child can use from the age of one year onwards. In nurseries and classrooms children have the opportunity of using many different types of blocks: from very large hollow ones that they can stand and climb on, to small ones such as Lego. Blocks can be hard and made out of wood or plastic, they can be soft and manufactured from rubber, cotton or foam, they can be brightly coloured or in natural wood – but they are all construction toys and are there to build with.

At first, children will play on their own, building a tower of bricks and enjoying knocking it down again. This leads on to four-year-old children planning small and large constructions together, playing cooperatively and imaginatively. In the establishment in which you are working, you will probably have wooden blocks that are all units of each other. For example, two rectangular blocks laid together horizontally will make a square, as will four of the small square blocks.

Understanding these relationships aids children in mathematical concepts, particularly those of fractions and of shape. The way the bricks are stored is important, and children will soon learn how many of the smaller bricks are equal to the larger ones.

The youngest children will use bricks to build towers and walls, enjoying the destruction as much or more than the building. Children of four and five will start to build, and often decide what their construction is as it takes shape. Older children will plan their constructions first, choose the most suitable materials and refer to resource material for inspiration and information. Seven year olds will use unit blocks to solve mathematical problems, and construction sets for developing and understanding technology.

Construction sets

There are many types of construction sets on the market, the best known being Lego. Most children will be familiar with Lego from home, and it is probably the most versatile of the construction toys. Younger children will find Duplo (the large-scale version) easier to put together. Older children, from five years upwards, enjoy Meccano, the wooden and plastic types being easier to manage than the metal, which is more sophisticated. There is an increasingly expanding market in construction sets, and you need to be assured of the value and versatility of each set before ordering.

Amount of space		Type of space		Type of play		Adult involvement	
Whole area		Outside	✔	Solitary	✔	Essential	
Half area		Inside	✔	Parallel	✔	Enriching	✔
Quarter area	✔	Hard surface	✔	Small group	✔	Not always necessary	✔
Small area	✔	Carpeted	✔	Large group	✔		
		Table space	✔			Can be intrusive	✔

Essential materials
- Bricks/blocks/construction sets and suitable storage.

Suggested additional materials
- Model cars, animals and people
- Blankets to make shelters
- Large cardboard cartons
- Paper and pencils to plan designs
- Photographs of buildings.

Links to the EYFS

Personal, social and emotional development
Cooperation is needed when planning and building constructions in a group. Children may have to share and take turns. An activity may involve an adult working alongside children. This is an enjoyable activity that promotes a sense of achievement and self-esteem. It has a home–school link. Children can have an outlet for aggression by banging and breaking down a construction. Building life-size models leads to a feeling of being in control.

Communication, language and literacy
Children have to understand and issue instructions when building together. Discussion of constructions with an adult will extend the children's positional language and learning. Planning constructions promotes negotiation. Older

▶

children will need to read and follow instructions in planning and building more sophisticated models, and using resource books will encourage literacy.

Problem solving, reasoning and numeracy

Building with bricks is a first-hand experience of three-dimensional objects and spatial relationships. Many mathematical concepts are learnt such as height, weight, matching, sorting and symmetry. It encourages concentration, creative thought and problem solving.

Knowledge and understanding of the world

Building with blocks and construction sets helps children understand the properties and functions of various materials.

Physical development

Large blocks promote good muscle development through lifting, carrying, stretching and balancing, while small bricks and construction sets aid gross and fine manipulative skills and hand–eye coordination.

Creative development

A well-designed construction is a creative experience and the beginning of an appreciation of architecture and design. Imagination is stimulated as children explore form and shape, as they plan and construct models. Construction sets are used to create other models, such as robots and aeroplanes. Polished wood gives a tactile experience.

Good practice: role of the adult

- Bricks and blocks should always be readily available for the children and stored somewhere they can reach for themselves. They must be kept in good condition and regularly checked for splinters. Plain wooden blocks will need to be varnished from time to time, especially if used outside. Plastic and foam blocks should be washed regularly. Construction sets need to be kept clean, and most are easy to wash. There need to be enough pieces, so that more than one child can play at the same time.
- Involve children in clearing away, so that they learn how to stack the blocks in the smallest possible space, as this will teach them how the sizes relate to each other. Labelling the area may help them. Smaller bricks and blocks can be usefully stored in large drawstring bags.
- Children benefit from building their constructions in a large area and, if possible, a carpeted part of the room should be kept for bricks and blocks. ▶

It may occasionally be possible to leave the work set up so that the children can return to it later. Staff need to realise that group building may take some time and to give ample warning before asking the children to clear away.

- Books showing pictures of buildings, machines, space equipment and forms of transport should be sited near the brick corner to aid the imagination.
- Adults should show sensitivity and understand when a child needs to work alone to solve problems, and anticipate when to offer help or extend the activity.

Essential points

Anti-discriminatory practice

- Boys often dominate the brick corner. Posters in this area depicting both genders involved in construction work should be displayed.
- Staff may need to actively encourage girls to use this area of the class, even occasionally excluding the boys for a session. The presence of an adult in the brick area will often encourage girls to participate.
- Children with special needs should have access to block play. Foam blocks are especially suitable. They may find it easier to play at a table and, if so, put a rug on the surface to prevent pieces slipping off.

Safety

- Large or heavy wooden blocks can be dangerous if thrown or allowed to topple onto other children.
- Wooden blocks need to be checked regularly for splinters.
- Small pieces from construction sets might make young children choke if they are put in the mouth.
- Plastic construction sets need to be washed regularly.

 ## Activity

Maintaining blocks and construction sets in good condition is an important part of your role.

- **How is this carried out in your placement?**
- **How often is the equipment washed?**

Partnership with parents

- Many children play with blocks at home, so parents will be familiar with this activity and this will also help new children to feel at home when they start nursery or school.

- Have a camera on hand to take photographs of the constructions so that parents can see finished work: these can be displayed.

Activity

Using catalogues, list the different types of bricks, blocks and construction sets available.

- Which types would you find the most appropriate for children with special needs?

- Which types would make the most complicated constructions?

Resources

Donati P., 1993, *Amazing Buildings*, Dorling Kindersley Ltd.

Evans D. and Williams C., 1993, *Building Things*, Let's Explore Science Series, Dorling Kindersley Ltd.

Gura P., 1992, *Exploring Learning: young children and block play*, Paul Chapman.

Heald C., 1997, *Construction Play*, Learning Through Play Series, Scholastic Publications Ltd.

Ross C. and Browne N., 1994, *Girls as Constructors in the Early Years*, Trentham Books.

Catalogue

Community Playthings (for address see General Resources, page 187) has excellent illustrations of many kinds of wooden blocks.

Websites

www.bobthebuilder.com

www.toy-testing.org

10 Puzzles and Table-top Activities

Jigsaw puzzles are familiar to most pre-school children, and create an excellent home–school link, as children feel relaxed and safe doing jigsaws when they first start at nursery. They are essentially a solitary experience, although children may do the large floor puzzles in a small group.

Jigsaws range from simple inset boards for the youngest children, to intricate puzzles for adults. Sometimes children will choose easy puzzles when they are feeling the need for reassurance and at other times they will enjoy the challenge of more demanding jigsaws. They are ideal for sick children, as they can be set up on a tray for those in bed. It is important that no pieces are missing, particularly for the younger children, as this spoils the pleasure of completing a task satisfactorily.

Board games similarly come in varying degrees of difficulty. Most are not suitable for the under fours as the children will not have yet gained the concept of taking turns, and may get upset at having to wait and spoil the game for others. Most games are a variation of Ludo or Snakes and Ladders.

Matching games, such as Picture Lotto and Connect, help children to see similarities and differences, and to match like with like. These can be played by one child alone, or with a group of children. Card games, such as Snap, Pairs or Sevens, are enjoyed by children of four years upwards. Snap or Pairs cards can be made quite easily, using pictures or photographs familiar to the children's cultural background. Ask permission before introducing packs of cards into your placement, as some establishments look on cards as an introduction to gambling.

Children enjoy threading beads and cotton reels, and again these are graded in order of difficulty, the younger children finding the larger beads the easiest. Pegboards and mosaic pieces help children to make patterns.

You might come across sewing cards, where children are asked to go in and out of holes with a lace or a threaded needle. Older children sometimes sew simple projects such as bookmarks or needle cases.

Amount of space		Type of space		Type of play		Adult involvement	
Whole area		Outside		Solitary	✔	Essential	
Half area		Inside	✔	Parallel	✔	Enriching	✔
Quarter area		Hard surface		Small group	✔	Not always necessary	✔
Small area	✔	Carpeted	✔	Large group		Can be intrusive	✔
		Table space	✔				

Essential materials

- Puzzles, board games, card games
- Beads
- Cotton reels
- Pegboards
- Mosaic pieces
- Sewing cards.

Links to the EYFS

Personal, social and emotional development

When played in groups, these toys and games involve children's turn-taking, cooperation and sharing. Games with rules aid understanding of society. Some games are competitive, and children have to learn to lose gracefully. Self-esteem is gained by the successful completion of puzzles. Patience and perseverance is needed.

Communication, language and literacy

Explaining and understanding instructions for games helps language development. It is necessary for children to learn to discriminate between letter and number symbols. If the game is on tape, children have to listen carefully.

Problem solving, reasoning and numeracy

Doing jigsaw puzzles and sorting and matching games helps children to find similarities and differences. Card games encourage memory and quickness of thought. Concentration, logical thought, reasoning and perseverance are necessary for all these activities. Many board games involve numbers, especially those that are played with dice. Number recognition, addition and subtraction may all be involved.

Knowledge and understanding of the world

Jigsaws and Picture Lotto can be linked to the natural world. They can also reflect life experiences and cultural celebrations. Children will gain by sharing such knowledge.

Physical development

All table toys are a great aid to developing gross and fine manipulative skills and the acquisition of precision movements. A tactile jigsaw is useful for a child with visual impairment.

Creative development

Colour, shape and patterns may be explored.

Activity

Describe which type of table-top game contributes most to the all-round development of the child.

✓ Good practice: role of the adult

- All equipment should be stored in strong boxes, to which the children have access and are allowed to select their own activity. Plastic equipment should be washed regularly.
- A good range and variety of puzzles should be available, to cater for all abilities and to allow choice. If there are pieces missing, the puzzle should be discarded, unless replacement pieces can be supplied.
- Card games and matching games should be complete.
- Other table top toys should be provided in sufficient quantity to allow a group to play together.
- Supervision may be necessary to make sure turns are taken fairly.

Essential points

Anti-discriminatory practice

- Equipment should reflect cultural diversity. For example, puzzles with pictures from around the world, depicting people of various ethnic origins, are available from most catalogues.
- Boys may need encouragement to sew.
- Several sets of photographic jigsaws should include children with disabilities.
- There are many games and puzzles available with raised features and various textures to encourage children with impairments to join in.

Safety

- Care needs to be taken with small beads and pegs with younger children, to make sure they are not swallowed or inserted into ears and noses.
- Blunt needles are quite satisfactory for sewing Binca material or felt, and are a useful way of encouraging children to be careful when they progress to using sharper ones.
- A clean, hazard-free floor area should be available for floor games and large puzzles.

Partnership with parents

- Parents might like to look at the range of equipment offered in the establishment, and may be invited to recommend games. The establishment might be able to lend a favourite game to a family, and this helps establish home–school links. Parents who volunteer to work in the classroom usually feel quite comfortable with table-top toys and jigsaws, as they are familiar with them.

Activity

Ask the children in your placement to help you to design and construct a board game for them. Bear in mind the ages of the children.

- Play the game with the children and write an evaluation of the activity.
- What did the children learn from your game?

Resources

Davies J., 1990, *Children's Games*, New edition, Piatkus Books.

Tavener J., 1998, *Table Top Games*, Learning Through Play Series, Scholastic Publications Ltd.

Games

Jigsaws for children with special needs are available from NES Arnold (for address see General Resources, page 187).

Websites

www.jigzone.com

www.compendia.co.uk

www.searchamateur.com

www.souperfun.com

www.afunzone.com

11 Books and Storytelling

Enjoyment of books and stories starts in the home. A child before the age of one year enjoys looking at pictures or photographs while being cuddled by an adult and read to. Nurturing this love of books is probably the key factor in the later acquisition of reading skills, which in turn leads to academic attainment and a lifelong pleasure in reading.

Young children in particular derive great pleasure from being told stories. These can be personalised, either being tales from the storyteller's past, or stories where the listener becomes the centre of the tale. Sometimes props can be used, such as puppets and flannelgraphs as, apart from making the story more vivid, they also help the child's memory when retelling the story. Flannelgraphs are pictures mounted on board. They tell the story and can be attached to a felt board one by one. They can be used with or without an adult. Some stories, such as *The Great Big Enormous Turnip*, lend themselves to flannelgraphs, as the story is simple and the characters are added in sequence.

Being told or read a story is delightful and relaxing. Many parents read to their children just before settling them down to sleep, and sick children benefit enormously from a familiar comforting story, and the sole attention of a loved adult.

Once a child starts school a great deal of emphasis is placed on learning to read. Parents are encouraged to come in to schools to hear children read, and take books home to continue the good work. Children often read in pairs, hearing each other, and practising their skills.

As a childcare and education practitioner, you will sometimes be reading to one or two children from a book of their choice, and you will be able to establish a close relationship. Children can participate in turning a page, placing pictures on a flannelgraph or lifting a flap. On other occasions you will be reading to a group of children, preferably all at a similar stage of development, and you will choose a book with the children where the pictures can be seen, and the story is age-appropriate. Reading to a group needs careful preparation beforehand.

Poetry will enrich children's vocabulary and let them know that it is acceptable to express emotions. This may encourage older children to write their own poems. For younger children humorous verse is a good introduction. Repetitive rhyming is most helpful to children with limited language skills. For all children, it can, like books, open up a world of fantasy and imagination.

Activity

Visit your local library.

- Is the children's section child-friendly and well stocked?
- Ask the librarian how they liaise with local schools and nurseries.
- Are special activities provided for children during the school holidays?

Amount of space	Type of space		Type of play		Adult involvement	
Whole area	Outside	✔	Solitary	✔	Essential	
Half area	Inside	✔	Parallel	✔	Enriching	✔
Quarter area	Hard surface		Small group	✔	Not always necessary	✔
Small area	✔	Carpeted	✔	Large group		Can be intrusive	
	Table space					

Essential materials

- A good range of books and stories, from picture books with no words to picture books with a very simple narrative: highly illustrated story books, bound books with a picture on every page, books with a longer narrative and some illustrations, information or resource books. There should be a balance of books that reflect a diversity of lifestyles, religions and cultures, and dilemmas that are faced by children, such as coping with divorce or a new baby in the family
- A comfortable, well-lit area for children to relax and read, and nearby storage.

Suggested additional materials

- Story sacks: sacks that contain the book and props relating to the story
- Puppets: glove, finger, string, paper, material
- Props: whatever is appropriate to the story, such as dolls, stuffed toys, cars and small world toys
- Flannelgraphs: characters and scenes from a book or story, which are made out of felt or a similar material, and will stick to a board as the story progresses
- Many familiar stories are now published in 'big book' form
- Access to a tape recorder
- Taped sounds or percussion music to accompany a story
- Taped stories, which the children can listen to themselves, together with the book. This is most successful when the story is taped by an adult they know, and they can hear themselves participating.

Links to the EYFS

Personal, social and emotional development

Reading in a small group is a cooperative sharing experience. Turns have to be taken when asking questions about the story and discussing the book. Respect must be learnt for the ideas of others. Many stories help children to discriminate between right and wrong. Other stories show children caring for each other.

Being able to read gives a child independence, self-esteem and a sense of achievement. Empathising with a character in a book allows a child to understand her own feelings. On a one-to-one basis, reading with an adult is a nurturing experience, giving feelings of love and security. It is a home–school link.

Communication, language and literacy

Books offer new vocabulary and foster listening skills. Repetitive stories and verse help those children with limited language. Children will understand that print carries meaning and this will encourage them to learn to read for themselves. Retelling stories helps develop memory and the ability to articulate ideas. Learning poetry and verse aids recall and memory, and often remains with you throughout life.

Problem solving, reasoning and numeracy

The concepts of size, number and sequencing can be explored in books and stories. One-to-one correspondence can be explored in stories such as *Goldilocks and the Three Bears*. There are many opportunities for counting.

Knowledge and understanding of the world

The ability to use information and resource material links in with all other activities. Books and stories encourage concentration and extend the child's knowledge of the world. Traditional stories and myths from many places can be included.

Physical development

Turning pages demands manipulative control. Sitting in a group to listen to a story needs physical control.

Creative development

Books can be a visual delight. Some books made today have buttons to press allowing areas of the book to light up or to make a noise. Others have areas to scratch to release a smell. Many are tactile, having pages with different textures to feel. Books will fire children's imagination and lead to creative and imaginative play. Attractive illustrations make children aware of the beauty of the world.

Activity

Visit a good children's bookshop in your area.

- List three books suitable for a six year old and three books for a three year old. Give reasons for your choice.
- Are there any other activities taking place in the bookshop, apart from the selling of books?
- During your visit, how many children were in the shop? Were they made welcome? Was there a place for them to sit and read?

Good practice: role of the adult

- In schools and pre-schools it is usual to have a book corner. This should be sited in a quiet area of the room, where there is not constant movement to and fro, in a good light, and with comfortable furniture, away from the messy or natural play area.

- Books should always be available to the children and, ideally, an adult always there to read to them if required. Children enjoy reading on the floor, so it is most important that this area is carpeted and kept clean. Books should be stored on shelves at the children's height, with some displayed on a table or on a rack so that children can see the covers. They should be kept in good condition, and children taught from a young age to treat them with respect. Books need inspecting for scribbles, torn or missing pages, or any other sort of damage, and should be removed if they cannot be repaired properly. Children who damage books should be encouraged to help in their repair. The display of books should be changed regularly, but favourite books should be left out as long as required. Books can be made by the children, and these are often highly valued.

- A comprehensive range of books needs to be available. The books should reflect our multicultural society, with stories from countries around the world and some books in the home languages of the children in the group. Great care must be taken to avoid stereotyping when choosing books. Positive images reflecting the diversity of culture and families today need to be included, together with stories portraying children with disabilities and girls in strong roles.

- Children identify with characters in books, and you should be aware of the needs of all the children in your group in order to help them make sense of their feelings and to promote self-esteem and feelings of worth. Children of all ages need information and factual books, linking in with other areas of their work, and to extend their experiences and knowledge.

- Remember the value of telling stories, as well as reading books. This is particularly valuable for the younger children, as the story you make up can be personalised with the names of the children in the group, and will therefore hold their interest more. Not all children like to be the centre of attention, so you need to be sensitive to this. Storytelling frees the hands so that you can use props to illustrate your story, and this helps children who may not yet be fluent in English to understand and participate more.

- For children to get the best from a group story, you need to think carefully about several things:

  1. The size of the group. Up to the age of four, six children should be the maximum number of two year olds and three year olds. It is important to maintain eye contact with these young children, so as to keep their interest and participation. Generally four year olds are able to concentrate in larger groups, but not all of them can do this, and you need to take the developmental age into account as well as how much experience the child has had of group stories.

  2. The appropriateness of the book or story needs thinking about. The youngest children will be content with stories about familiar events, such as shopping and bedtime, and some simple tales that are happily resolved about other children and animals. As children's experience of stories is extended, longer books about imaginary events can be read,

but always be aware of frightening the children. Young children's imagination is very vivid, and fairy stories can be terrifying, as they often deal with tales of rejection and separation. Ogres and witches should be left for an older age group, and even then not all children feel comfortable with fantasy tales, as they may still have difficulty in discriminating fact from fiction.

3. The way that you read stories has a good deal of bearing on how much the children will enjoy them. Your voice should not be dull and monotonous, and you should try to cultivate different tones and pitches for dialogue. You should choose stories you enjoy reading and telling, and you will need to be familiar with the story you are going to read. If you are asked to read a story you dislike, this may show in your delivery of it.

- Timing is important. It is futile to expect children to gain a great deal from a story session if it is placed just before lunchtime, when hungry children are distracted by the smell of food and interrupted by being told to go and wash their hands. To read to them just before home time, when the children are tired and falling asleep, and distracted by parents arriving to collect them is also a wasted opportunity. Children who have not really settled into the group will not listen to a word, as they are anxiously watching the door and waiting to be collected. Far better to read stories in the middle of working sessions, when the children have no expectations of immediately seeing loved adults, and are not too tired and hungry to concentrate.

- Not all young children are ready to sit in a group, and a quiet alternative activity should be allowed until the child wants to join in. All other activities in the pre-school are voluntary, and sitting with a group for any reason should be as well.

- Children tend to want the same stories time and time again, but occasionally you need to introduce new stories. Sometimes it is a good idea to leave the book on the display table for a little while first, so that the children can familiarise themselves with the pictures.

- Some books have many words in them that are unfamiliar to the children. It is not a good idea to change the words into more familiar ones as you go along. This is disrespectful to the writer, and it deprives the children of learning new words. If the language is so difficult that the children become bored, reintroduce the book another time with older children.

- Allow some time for relaxed discussion at the end of the story. Children do not always want to talk about the book, so do not force them to do so. Sometimes children want to participate throughout the reading or telling of the story. It depends on your personal preference as to whether you let them do this or wait until the end of the story session. Usually the youngest children cannot wait until the end if they have something to say!

- Other adults might want to be involved in story time. Sometimes parents will read to a small group of children, and this is particularly useful if you ▶

have bilingual children in your class. Reading sessions are sometimes held in your local library, or the librarian will come into the school to read to the children. Older children should be encouraged to join the library, and the younger ones should be familiar with the building.

- Books should represent the whole spectrum of society, not just the ideal nuclear family with no financial problems.
- When buying new books, or borrowing books from the library, care must be taken to make sure that none of them contain elements that could offend adults or distress children, by displaying offensive attitudes.
- Show children that you enjoy books, as it is by your example that they will learn to value and appreciate books and stories. Remember that books have a place in most of the activities and experiences of the children, and always be ready to provide the appropriate book when the occasion demands.

Wendy Ewer has devised a checklist (see pages 101–2), which may be useful when selecting books to use with children.

CHECKLIST FOR BOOKS AND STORIES

Name _____

Date _____ Age of children _____ No. of children _____

Title _____ Author _____

Publisher _____ ISBN _____

Type of book: Fact/Fiction/Picture book/Poetry/Rhyme

1 My choice of book/story was agreed with _____

2 I presented the book by reading/ by telling/ with a visual aid

3 I prepared, before sharing the book, by _____
   _____

4 (a) The place was suitable because _____
   _____

   (b) The children and adults were comfortable because _____
   _____

   (c) All the children could see because _____

   (d) I settled the children for the session by _____
   _____

5 The story was suitable for the children's age, level of development,
   concentration and interest because _____
   _____

6 (a) I made eye contact with the child/ren _____
   _____

   (b) I used different voice tones and volume for _____
   _____

7 I dealt with (interruptions or distractions) _____
_____

8 The children participated by _____

9 The children's comments were _____
_____

And I responded by _____
_____

10 I engaged their attention and helped their concentration by _____
_____

11(a) I finished the session by _____
_____
_____

(b) The children reacted to the story/book by _____
_____

12 The book reflected positive images by _____
_____

13 I could use this story/book again with _____
_____

Comments _____
_____
_____
_____
_____
_____

I verify that the candidate has read/told/shared this story/book as
stated above.

Signed _____

Essential points

Anti-discriminatory practice

- Books are an ideal way of presenting positive images of children from many varied ethnic groups. By giving all children insight into different cultures with their own traditional stories and into varied child-rearing practices, they will learn to value and respect people for who they are, and to challenge stereotypical attitudes. Check the books' illustrations for stereotypes. Make sure that children with special needs are not depicted as being weak and needy.
- There should be books in home languages so that all parents can read to their children in the classroom, and the value attached to this can be seen by other children. Some books are published in dual texts.
- Girls should be depicted in strong roles, not as dependent, passive onlookers.
- Noise levels should be kept down so that all children can hear and be heard.
- Books should be available to help children who have to deal with problems in their private lives, such as hospitalisation, parental separation, bereavement and so on.
- There should be a selection of books depicting children with special needs as central characters in a story.
- Books that can be read in English and in sign language are available. Tactile books can be purchased or made for visually impaired children and for very young children.

Safety

- Books do not present a hazard, but care should be taken when using story props that small pieces are not inserted or ingested.

Partnership with parents

- **Books are an obvious home–school link and most parents read regularly with and to their children. Parents wishing to help in establishments are usually very comfortable helping hear children read and reading to a small group of children. Many schools send books home with the children and invite parents to comment on the children's progress. There are often workshops in schools to explain the literacy hour and to expound on the value of books.**

Resources

Dorling Kindersley, 2004, *My First Word Board Book*, Dorling Kindersley.

Drifte C., 2003, *Literacy Play for the Early Years* (series of 4 books), David Fulton.

Fitzsimmons J. and Whiteford R., 1995, *English Key Stage 1*, Blueprints Series, 2nd edition, Nelson Thornes.

James F. and Kerr A., 1993, *On First Reading*, Belair Publications.

Magee Wes, 1992, *Poetry Compilation*, Scholastic Publications Ltd.

Milord S., 2007, *Tales Alive*, Williamson Publishing.

Mukherji P. and O'Dea T., 2000, *Understanding Children's Language and Literacy*, Nelson Thornes Ltd.

Rosen M., 1994, *A World of Poetry*, Kingfisher.

Anthologies

Doherty B., 2002, *Fairy Tales*, 2nd edition, Walker Books.

Harrison M. and Stuart-Clark C., 2000, *The Oxford Treasury of World Stories*, OUP.

Morpurgo M. and Sandburg R., 2006, *The Kingfisher Treasury of Classic Stories*, Kingfisher Books Ltd.

Websites

www.bbc.co.uk/cbeebies/stories

www.enchantedlearning.com/rhymes.htm

www.candlelightstories.com

www.penguin.com

www.literacytrust.org.uk

www.amazon.co.uk

Bookshops and book associations

Africa Book Centre Ltd, Preston Park Business Centre, 36 Robertson Road, Brighton BN1 5NL. Telephone: 01273 560 474. Website: www.africabookcentre.com

Bookspread, 6 Croxted Road, London, SE21 8SW. Telephone: 0845 200 4954.

The Centre for Language in Primary Education, www.clpe.co.uk/index.html.

Letterbox Library, 71–73 Allen Road, Stoke Newington, London N16 8RY. Telephone: 020 7503 4801.

Society for Storytelling, http://sfs.org.uk/.

Working Group against Racism in Children's Resources, Unit 34 Eurolink Business Centre, 49 Effra Road, London SW2 1BZ. Telephone: 0207 501 9992. Website: www.wgarcr.org.uk

12 Music, Sound and Movement

Music is a familiar part of everybody's life. Some people think that foetuses respond to music in the womb. It seems to have a calming effect and is even attributed to linking neurons in the brain, promoting intelligence.

From a very young age, babies will respond without discrimination but with enjoyment to a wide range of musical and rhythmic sounds. Lullabies are often used to soothe babies to sleep. As children grow older, their musical taste is formed by outside influences, particularly those of the family, the culture they are born into, the media, and their primary carers and peers.

It seems entirely natural to move in response to rhythm, and moving to music and dancing is enjoyed throughout life, by children and adults within all cultures.

Experimenting with musical instruments and singing helps children discriminate sounds and aids their language development. In some classrooms and homes, singing or rhyming is quite natural, and carries on between the children and adults as a way of normal communication.

Activities

- Visit a local music shop. What tapes, CDs and sheet music do they have that is suitable for young children?
- List the range of instruments to which the children have access in your placement.
- Compile a repertoire of songs that you could sing with the children.

Amount of space		Type of space		Type of play		Adult involvement	
Whole area	✔	Outside	✔	Solitary		Essential	
Half area	✔	Inside	✔	Parallel		Enriching	✔
Quarter area	✔	Hard surface	✔	Small group	✔	Not always necessary	✔
Small area		Carpeted	✔	Large group	✔	Can be intrusive	✔
		Table space					

Essential equipment

- Repertoire of songs and rhymes, and the confidence to sing them
- Space for movement.

Suggested additional equipment

- Record, DVD, CD or cassette player all with headphones
- Range of records, CDs and cassette tapes, containing music and sounds from around the world, incorporating all musical styles
- Tape recorder
- A range of good quality percussion instruments, such as shakers, Chinese wood claps, Indian dancer's bells and steel drums
- Stringed instrument played by a member of staff
- Instruments made by the children
- Simple wind instruments, such as Indian pipes and Irish penny whistles
- Piano
- Resource books.

Links to the EYFS

Personal, social and emotional development

Music is an opportunity to share experiences and to provide a musical introduction to diverse cultures. It is a non-competitive activity, and helps build relationships. Children have to learn to share and take turns, and to have consideration for others. Music encourages freedom of expression, and the release of emotions such as pleasure, fear and frustration. It can be relaxing and therapeutic, and can raise self-esteem and confidence, especially in older children, when performing. Music and songs from all cultures will help children to develop positive feelings of acceptance and a sense of belonging, and this also encourages respect.

Communication, language and literacy

Singing develops expressive language, articulation, vocabulary, diction and expressive use of the voice. Music develops listening skills and heightens a feeling for language, exploring a new means of expression.

Problem solving, reasoning and numeracy

Music aids memory, concentration, sequencing, classification and discrimination. There should be opportunities to match and copy sounds and movement.

Knowledge and understanding of the world

Children will be interested in volume and vibration, and in exploring how and why sounds change, and in exploring the properties of various instruments.

Physical development

Moving to music and using instruments develops body and spatial awareness, balance, coordination and agility. Playing instruments and executing finger rhymes helps develop fine manipulative skills and hand–eye coordination. Hearing is sharpened by the practice of discriminating sounds. Touch is stimulated by handling well-made instruments.

Creative development

Music and movement can be an aesthetic and spiritual experience, and is often uplifting.

✔ *Good practice: role of the adult*

- Music should always be available to children. A music table set up with a selection of good quality instruments and those made by the children should stand in an accessible area of the room. Instruments should be changed regularly, in the same way as are books in the book corner. Children need to be shown how to treat instruments with respect, but if any are damaged they should be removed for repair. The youngest children have the keenest hearing and therefore should always have access to the best instruments that can be provided.

- Occasionally there should be a time when the children can listen to some music that they might not otherwise come across, such as music from different parts of the world, electronic sound patterns, operatic arias, rap or modern jazz. Apart from being a relaxing experience, it extends the children's musical appreciation and knowledge.

- There should be music sessions at least once a day. These should be very short for the youngest children – 10 minutes is quite enough. They do not have to be directed by a music specialist and all that is required of you in organising the session is a constantly updated repertoire of suitable songs and rhymes, and the confidence to lead the session in a lively and enthusiastic manner. Although it will distance you from the children, it adds a great deal to the musicality of the session if you are able to play an instrument, such as a guitar or the piano. These instruments will leave your voice free for singing, but if this talent is not available a record or a tape will do almost as well. You should offer familiar songs and activities, as well as introducing new ones. Actions and movements designed to go with songs and rhymes help children concentrate, offer enjoyment and motivation, and help them to interpret music with their bodies.

- At certain times during the day, when the noise will not interfere with other, quieter activities, children should be encouraged to experiment with the instruments available in making their own music. The adult should be on hand to help them with this improvisation.

- Not all music sessions require instruments. Just singing songs that appeal to children is an enjoyable and worthwhile experience. Sometimes children might have access to a large space such as the school hall, and moving to rhythmic patterns that can be clapped by hand or beaten out on a percussion instrument helps children to move in a controlled way. On other occasions, some loud music for dancing will allow self-expression and release of tension, in vigorous physical exercise.

- Remember not to have music playing constantly in the background. This will deaden children's discrimination.

Essential points

Anti-discriminatory practice

- Be aware of gender and racial stereotypes in songs and rhymes. It is probably better to discard such songs, rather than alter the words. Take children to see neighbourhood festivals, with performances by professional dancers or musicians, as well as local performers.
- Music allows children who do not speak English to join in and participate, as music is international. This aids speech and language development.
- Every culture has its own musical traditions and instruments, such as the flute in Irish music and the steel drums in African-Caribbean rhythms. Children should be introduced to a wide variety of musical traditions.
- Use songs and records or tapes in various languages, and in different musical styles. Ask parents and staff to teach the children the songs they grew up with, remembering there are many different European cultures too. Collect musical instruments from various cultures.
- Children with disabilities will find simple, repetitive songs and rhymes relaxing and soothing. All children enjoy playing percussion instruments, and special grip pads and stands are available. Children with hearing impairments enjoy listening to the vibrations of low-pitched sounds. Visually impaired children need highly developed hearing skills to compensate for poor vision. Instruments can be suspended so that they can be played with one hand. Movement to music on a one-to-one basis can be particularly useful for children with multiple disabilities. Some music calms children with behavioural difficulties.

Safety

- Very young children need careful supervision, particularly when playing with home-made instruments.
- Very loud music played constantly can damage hearing.
- The movement area should be clean, safe and free from hazards.

Activity

Plan a music or a movement activity for (a) three year olds and (b) five year olds. How will the approach, the equipment and the adult's role vary?

 ## *Partnership with parents*

- Another good home–school link.
- Some parents may play an instrument and be willing to come into the school or nursery to play for the children. Others may have interesting tapes or CDs that they are willing to lend.
- Music is often the basis for the annual school concert where parents enjoy watching their children perform and can occasionally be persuaded to take part in making costumes, making up the children and helping them rehearse.

Resources

Drew H., 1993, *My First Music Book*, Dorling Kindersley Ltd.

Evans D. and Williams C., 1993, *Let's Explore Science; Sound and Music*, Dorling Kindersley Ltd.

Foster J. and Thompson C., 2002, *Chanting Rhymes*, OUP.

Harrison L., 1998, *Dance and Drama*, Learning Through Play Series, Scholastic Publications Ltd.

Harrop B., Friend L. and Gadsby D., 1995, *Okki-tokki-unga*, A.&C. Black (Publishers) Ltd.

Macintyre C., 2002, *Early Intervention in Movement*, David Fulton.

Macintyre C., 2003, *Jingle Time*, David Fulton.

McKellar S., 1993, *Counting Rhymes*, Dorling Kindersley Ltd.

Matterson E., 2002, *This Little Puffin*, Revised edition, Puffin Books.

Merry K., 1993, *Big, Big Multi-cultural Music Book*, New edition, Merry Publications.

Opie I. and P., 1970, *The Puffin Book of Nursery Rhymes*, Puffin Books.

Pound L. and Harrison C., 2002, *Supporting Musical Development in the Early Years*, OUP.

Whiteford R., 1991, *Music and Movement*, Bright Ideas for Early Years Series, Scholastic Publications Ltd.

Wilkes A., 1992, *Animal Nursery Rhymes*, Dorling Kindersley Ltd.

Young S., 2003, *Music with the Under Fours*, RoutledgeFalmer.

Catalogue

Acorn Percussion, Unit 34, Abbey Business Centre, Ingate Place, London SW8 3NS. Telephone: 0207 627 3020.

Websites

http://richardsinstitute.org

www.mindinst.org

www.youthmusic.co.uk

www.music-at-school.co.uk

13 Outside Play

Nearly every activity that takes place in the classroom or nursery can equally well happen outside if the weather permits. Some activities have to take place outside, however, and it is to these that this chapter refers.

A safe outside play area is vital for young children, to exercise and let off steam, to practise their developing physical skills and to build self-confidence. Some children have limited access to safe outdoor play at home and need fresh air and exercise to promote good health.

A safe outdoor play area allows children freedom to investigate and explore their environment with little adult restriction. It should be an integral part of the pre-school provision and, ideally, children should have access to it at all times. This should be taken into account when planning activities, always remembering that outside play should not be compulsory, any more than any other activity. Young children who are not used to playing outside may find the playground intimidating and overwhelming at first, but when their self-confidence has developed they will soon enjoy being outside if allowed to choose for themselves.

Ideally, in an outside play area attached to a pre-school establishment or a school there should be space and storage for wheeled toys, a grass area, an area for gardening, some trees and bushes to give shelter and privacy, and a surface suitable for the securing of climbing equipment and slides.

The playground must be effectively supervised and safety aspects taken into account. What is provided will influence the quality of the play. The presence of an enthusiastic adult, who joins in the children's play, rather than just standing outside with a cup of tea, will ensure maximum enjoyment and extend physical development. Traditional games may be organised, either by the children, or by an adult, such as 'What's the Time, Mr Wolf?', 'Hide and Seek' and 'Ring-O'-Roses'. Children in the infant school often take part in clapping games and skipping activities. Obviously, children should not be pressurised into taking part if they do not wish to.

Amount of space		Type of space		Type of play		Adult involvement	
Whole area	✔	Outside	✔	Solitary	✔	Essential	
Half area		Inside		Parallel	✔	Enriching	✔
Quarter area		Hard surface		Small group	✔	Not always necessary	✔
Small area		Carpeted		Large group	✔	Can be intrusive	
		Table space					

Essential equipment

- Outside area
- Storage facility
- Protective and warm clothing, such as spare Wellingtons, gloves and hats; sun hats and sun block.

Suggested additional equipment

- Large equipment, which might include a climbing frame, planks, galvanised metal A-frames, barrels and a slide
- Large covered containers for natural materials, such as sand and water
- Benches for sitting on
- Large cardboard cartons; wooden and plastic crates; tyres; tree trunks; cubes with holes
- Trampolines; ladders; tunnels; drainpipes, plastic guttering, pieces of hosepipe
- Pails and large brushes for 'painting' paving stones and walls with water
- Patch of ground for the cultivation of flowers and quick growing vegetables; gardening equipment such as trowels and small forks, watering cans, flower pots; bird table
- Place reserved for making mud pies
- Bicycles, scooters and other wheeled toys, which can be used by more than one child, such as hay carts, porter's trolleys, pushchairs and articulated push-alongs
- Small equipment such as pulleys, ropes, quoits, bats, balls and beanbags, blankets and magnifying glasses
- It is fun to use chalk outside, but some placements feel it may lead to children writing graffiti.

Links to the EYFS

Personal, social and emotional development

Children share, take turns and collaborate, take responsibility for sharing space, and gain understanding of the rules governing outside play and games. Friendships develop and children learn respect for living things. Outside play is enjoyable, releasing tension and aggression, and gives freedom from restriction. Challenging play leads to self-confidence and self-esteem, and gives children power over the environment. It allows some children to succeed who may not shine academically.

Communication, language and literacy

Outside play develops the use and understanding of vocabulary, in particular spatial terms. Children learn the language of the playground, including traditional playground rhymes. The games devised by some children have to be communicated clearly and carefully to the others.

Problem solving, resoning and numeracy

Outside play encourages concentration and powers of observation. It helps children to understand concepts of height, width, speed, distance, growth and spatial relationships. Children can be given some responsibility for planning and decision making.

Knowledge and understanding of the world

Children learn to observe the wonders of nature, such as rainbows, reflections in puddles, birds, animals and insects, growing plants and changing seasons. They start to estimate different speeds as they run or use the wheeled toys. There may be the opportunity to solve problems, for example when some of the equipment does not work properly.

Physical development

Playing outside releases surplus energy and is a licence to make more noise. It stimulates the appetite, aids digestion and circulation, promotes sleep and gives resistance to infection. It promotes healthy skin, as well as developing muscle tone, manipulative skills, balance and control. Children develop skills, such as stopping and starting, running, hopping, digging, planting, skipping, climbing, pedalling, swinging, steering, crawling through and under equipment and carrying.

Creative development

The outside area provides a stimulus for all the senses and an opportunity for a range of imaginary play experiences.

Good practice: role of the adult

- The successful outside play area needs careful planning, so that the children can play as freely as possible without being run over by wheeled toys or hit on the head by footballs. The equipment should be linked to the ages and stages of the children, so that the younger children are not put at risk, but there is challenging equipment for the older ones. If the age range is very wide, you may need to have separate areas for the babies and for the older children.

- Children should help to plan the outside play, by taking turns to choose the equipment, and should also help set it out and put it away. There should be a breadth and a balance in the outdoor curriculum, taking into account the needs of all the children, the older ones needing more complex play, such as assault courses, and the newcomers able to try out new skills without interference.

- Inside and outside play should be freely available, and neither area should be compulsory in the pre-school.

- Toys that can be used only by one child at a time, such as bicycles, can cause more trouble than they are worth, and adults need to supervise. Seen as representing power, children are often reluctant to share, and quarrels ensue over whose turn it is and how long someone has been on the bike. On the other hand, they give the opportunity of acquiring skills such as balance, steering and pedalling, not available to some children.

- Adults should enjoy and be involved in outside play, not just passively supervising. The area needs to be kept clean, and all equipment washed and serviced regularly.

- Children must be dressed according to the weather, protected against the sun as well as the rain.

- There is a need for resource books, so that amateur gardeners and scientists can have their questions answered.

- Parents must be informed of any accidents and details recorded in the accident book.

Activity

Plan a simple assault course for pre-school children. What equipment would you use? What would make it more challenging?

Essential points

Anti-discriminatory practice

- It has been observed that boys tend to dominate outside play and the use of the equipment. Measures can be taken to redress the balance by, for example, allowing only the girls to use the wheeled toys for one session, or see that they have access first.
- Guard against having expectations of children's physical abilities based on stereotypes.
- Parents could be asked for suggestions for games from all cultures, to reflect diversity.
- For children with disabilities, soft play equipment such as foam-filled large blocks can be provided. Games should generally be non-competitive although some individual children might enjoy an element of competition. Plastic bats and a variety of balls can be used. Bean bags are easier to control than bouncing balls.
- Velcro straps can be fitted to bicycle pedals and some climbing equipment can be adapted, perhaps with bars across.
- Visually impaired children see white balls more clearly than coloured balls.

Safety

- Potentially, this is a dangerous area and children must have the rules of safety carefully explained and demonstrated to them. These need constant reinforcing. You need to remember, if supervising hearing impaired children, that they will not hear shouted warnings.
- Check the outside area for broken glass, undesirable objects and dog mess before allowing children to play. Check all large equipment routinely, for splinters and stability, and make sure that all the joints, nuts and screws are correctly in place. If faulty, take the piece of equipment out of use and report it immediately.
- Ensure that the equipment is serviced regularly by, for example, polishing and oiling. All new equipment must be fixed securely, must meet health and safety standards, and must be purchased from a recognised reputable firm. A first aid box should be easily accessible.
- The area under any climbing equipment should be soft and durable, using bark chippings or rubberised tiles.
- Access to the slide should be only by the stairs, and children should come down feet first, not head first.
- Climbing equipment should never be used when wet, and needs drying well after rain before using again. This sort of equipment needs constant supervision and alertness on your part. Children should not be allowed to climb in clothes that trail behind them, in tight jeans that restrict movement

▶

or in unsuitable shoes such as those in the dressing-up box, rubber sandals or flip flops.

- There should be as few rules as possible, but these must be strictly adhered to by both children and adults.
- Assault courses are fun and challenging for children, but also need close supervision.
- Sand pits need to be kept covered when not in use so that animals cannot get in. Sand must be swept up when spilt, sieved and washed before putting back.
- Seesaws and rocking boats should be in a safe place and not rock into a wall or the sand pit. Care must be taken to see that hands do not get trapped underneath.
- Swings are dangerous unless carefully supervised and in an area with a fence around.
- The whole of the playground should be visible to the adult. The boundary wall should be high enough to discourage children climbing on it, and to prevent access to strangers. Gates and doors should be kept locked.
- Bins for rubbish should be kept in a separate place.

Activity

Ask to look in the accident book in your placement.

- Identify the accidents that have occurred in the outside play area.
- Is there any particular area where accidents are more frequent?
- How could any of these accidents been avoided?

When choosing plants for the outside area you should be aware that the following species are known to be poisonous: arum lily, autumn crocus, castor oil plant, cherry laurel, daphne, datura (angel's trumpets), deadly nightshade, foxglove, glory lily, hellebore, ivy, laburnum, lantana, leopard lily, lily of the valley, monkshood, oleander, poisonous primula, rue, spurge and yew.

Partnership with parents

- Make parents aware that children may make their clothes dirty when playing outside. For safety, shoes need to be sensible, and long skirts or trailing cords can be dangerous.
- Parents have a right to be informed if there is an accident, and to see it recorded in the accident book.
- It is just as important to inform parents of how a child is acquiring physical skills as it is in reporting academic progress.

Activity

List five types of outdoor play, and give examples of equipment that could be used to extend each type.

Resources

Bilton H., 2002, *Outdoor Play in the Early Years*, 2nd edition, David Fulton.

De Boo M., 1992, *Action Rhymes and Games*, Bright Ideas for Early Years Series, Scholastic Publications Ltd.

Eustice V. and Heald C., 1992, *Outdoor Play*, Bright Ideas for Early Years Series, Scholastic Publications Ltd.

Filer J., 2008, *Healthy, Active and Outside!*, David Fulton.

Heddle R. and Shipton P., 1993, *Science with Weather*, Science Activities Series, Usborne Publishing.

Opie I. and Opie O., 1984, *Children's Games in Street and Playground*, OUP.

Ouvry M., 2003, *Exercising Muscles and Minds*, National Children's Bureau.

Readman J., 1993, *Muck and Magic*, Search Press with the Henry Doubleday Research Association.

Sutcliffe M., 1993, *Physical Education Activities and Outdoor Play*, Bright Ideas for Early Years Series, Scholastic Publications Ltd.

Unwin M., 1992, *Science with Plants*, Science Activities Series, Usborne Publishing.

Wilkes A., 1992, *My First Garden Book*, Dorling Kindersley Ltd.

Catalogue

Community Playthings (for address see General Resources, page 187).

Websites

www.whitehutchinson.com

www.ltl.org.uk

Organisations

Learning through Landscapes. Telephone: 01962 845 811.

Royal Horticultural Society, www.rhs.org.uk/Learning/Education.

Local wildlife trusts.

14 Outings

Children you are working with will have a wide variety of different experiences, and this will include their knowledge of the outside world. Some children are quite familiar with airports and holidays abroad, some may be lucky enough to enjoy different weekly outings with their family, but others may come from families where there is no money for the extra luxuries of transport and admission charges, and working adults may have little energy to take their children to new situations and enjoy new experiences with them.

Outings are important as a means of widening the children's environment and making them aware of other people's roles and the structure of the community in which they live. However broad their experience, children do not often have the opportunity to go for a walk at their own pace, to have questions patiently answered and to respond to questions put to them.

In the pre-school setting, it is not necessary to be too ambitious. A walk to the park to feed the birds, to the letterbox to post a letter (and await its arrival at the nursery the next day), to the supermarket to shop for cooking ingredients or to the station to watch the trains arrive and leave are all enriching experiences.

As children progress through infant school, outings can become more structured, and can include a visit to a swimming pool, a local farm, a zoo, a building site, the market place in the local community and a concert in church halls. Most art galleries are quite suitable for five year olds to give them their first exposure to art, and many museums have a creative development area for young children. By seven or eight most children are ready for visits to all museums and art galleries, as long as the outing is kept quite short, and just one particular display is targeted.

Some schools and day care centres may take all the children, staff and parents on a grand annual outing to the seaside or a theme park. Whilst very good for staff–parent relationships, it is difficult to give the children the same individual attention as you would be able to do on a less ambitious outing.

Outings are a useful way to introduce a theme or project to a class of five, six or seven year olds to link with the Foundation or National Curriculum.

Amount of space	Type of space		Type of play		Adult involvement	
Whole area	Outside	✔	Solitary		Essential	✔
Half area	Inside		Parallel		Enriching	✔
Quarter area	Hard surface		Small group	✔	Not always necessary	
Small area	Carpeted		Large group	✔		
	Table space				Can be intrusive	

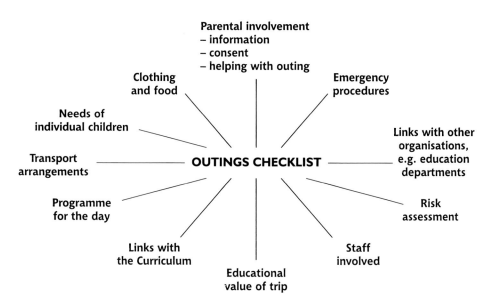

Parental involvement
– information
– consent
– helping with outing

Clothing and food

Emergency procedures

Needs of individual children

Links with other organisations, e.g. education departments

Transport arrangements

OUTINGS CHECKLIST

Programme for the day

Risk assessment

Links with the Curriculum

Staff involved

Educational value of trip

Essential equipment

- First aid equipment
- Form of identification
- Appropriate clothing and sensible shoes
- Tissues
- Written permission from parents
- Money
- Mobile phone.

Suggested additional equipment

- A bag for collecting 'treasures' (if going on a nature walk)
- Small games equipment (if going to the park)
- Swimming costumes and towels (if going swimming)
- Paper and pens (if going to a museum or art gallery)
- Lunch (if going to be out for the day)
- Spare clothing in case of accidents
- Wet wipes
- Emergency money.

Links to the EYFS

Personal, social and emotional development

Outings are a great social experience, going somewhere together as a group, with children, staff and parents involved. They provide opportunities for children to talk and relate to other children, and may lead to new friendships. There are many safety rules that have to be learnt and understood when going out together. Everyone has to behave responsibly. Outings are fun, and can offer a release from the routine existence of school. They give children confidence and self-esteem.

Communication, language and literacy

Outings offer opportunities for discussion, questions, conversations and new vocabulary.

Problem solving, reasoning and numeracy

Children can note the distance they have travelled and realise how important it is to be able to count, as adults are constantly checking that all the children are there! Children are often given maps of the place visited and can work out which art room they are in or in which area to find particular animals.

Knowledge and understanding of the world

Outings offer knowledge of the outside world, and usually lead to much follow-up work being carried out, in all areas of the curriculum. Children sometimes take part in the planning and are exposed to new places, ideas and experiences.

Physical development

Outings provide opportunities for fresh air and exercise, as in outside play. Walking strengthens leg muscles. Swimming tones up the whole body, and is an introduction to a form of exercise that will give pleasure throughout life.

Creative development

This will vary from outing to outing. Most outings, particularly nature walks and visits to art galleries, inspire creativity in the children.

✓ Good practice: role of the adult

- The younger the children, the simpler the outing, the shorter the journey, the smaller the number of children and the greater ratio of adults to children are good rules to remember. Young children of two and three do not enjoy being in confined areas such as museums and theatres, and have the rest of their lives to enjoy them.
- Some visits have very little educational value. For example, what is a visit to a store's grotto to see Father Christmas teaching the children? That it is quite all right to sit on an old man's knee and ask for presents? Outings like this please adults. They are the ones who don't mind sitting for two hours in a ▶

coach to see the lights in a London street, whereas the children will probably have fallen asleep before getting there, and have a very limited view of the lights at best. Outings like these are all right for parents to take their own children, but totally unsuitable for group outings.

Before the outing:

- Discuss where you are thinking of going with the team and head of the establishment.
- If possible, before making arrangements, visit the venue to check on opening times, safety, travel routes and facilities, such as lavatories and refreshment areas. If you are accompanied by a child or an adult in a wheelchair, you will need to check for wheelchair accessibility.
- Discuss the forthcoming visit with a person in charge of the venue. Do they have an educational department? If possible, get hold of some literature. Check that the insurance of the establishment covers the particular outing you have in mind. For example, travelling in private transport may need special insurance cover.
- Inform the parents and ask them to sign consent forms. Display notices with information about the outing around the school or nursery, giving departure and return times, funding for the trip and general information. If lunch is to be provided by the parents, involve them in planning a suitable picnic lunch.
- If any parent is unable to make a contribution to the cost of the trip, the school/nursery fund will often help by paying for the child to go. This must be done in strict confidence.
- Make sure you have enough adults to enforce the rules of safety: for example, you should have one adult for every two pre-school children, and one adult for every four infant school children. Volunteering adults may need some clear guidelines on how to deal with difficult or challenging behaviour.
- Prepare children for the outing. Show them leaflets and posters if possible, and read them stories. Talk to them about what they are going to see and do, and stress the safety rules.

On the day:

- Check the travel facilities.
- Make sure you have your first aid kit, any essential medication, spare clothing, spare food for lunch (in case anyone has left theirs behind), equipment for the day, towels and tissues in case of accidents, emergency money and a mobile phone. A camera could be taken to be shared by the older children.
- Remember that the children will need close supervision at all times.
- For younger children, a badge or label should be secured on their clothing, giving the name and telephone number of the nursery but not the name of the child, or any address. Safety rules need to be repeated at the start of the outing.
- Encourage the children to participate, explore and observe, and, where appropriate, to collect items. Your enthusiasm will encourage the children to ▶

enjoy themselves. Worksheets should be provided for six to seven year olds, where the outing is part of work within the National Curriculum.

- Any children likely to be over-exuberant or anxious should be looked after by a member of staff, not someone unfamiliar with them. All children have needs and the adults looking after the children should be sensitive to this.
- Children should not carry a lot of money or bring anything personal that would cause distress if it was lost.

After the outing:

- The older children should be asked to record their experiences in some way, and while younger children might volunteer to express their pleasure in the outing in a drawing, this should not be expected.
- The follow-up work may include, after some discussion, a variety of artwork, writing stories, poems or factual accounts, making a display, providing objects for an interest table and a book of photographs. Younger children may begin to incorporate some of the experiences into their role play.

Activity

Describe an outing that you think would be very suitable for three-year-old children, and give your reasons.

Essential points

Anti-discriminatory practice

- Outings offer opportunities to visit places of worship of many religions, museums displaying artefacts from many places and art galleries showing art from many cultures.
- Children might have the opportunity to join in local celebrations and festivals that may offer an insight into our diverse society. They might also visit a variety of shops and markets selling food from around the world.
- Outings may offer an opportunity for children to be looked after by a person from another culture or ethnic group.
- Not all outings are gender-free, but children should be encouraged to enjoy a wide variety of experiences and opportunities.
- If you have children with special needs in your group, they will benefit greatly from an outing, so you must make sure that there is proper access and comfortable travel arrangements. They may need more help and support, and may require the sole attention of one adult.
- Sometimes visits can be especially chosen to stimulate children with a sensory impairment, for example a visit to a children's zoo would allow them to touch, hear, see and smell the animals. The sense of smell will be greatly stimulated by a visit to the baker's – or the local farm!

Safety

- Before the outing, check the area for potential hazards and discard the venue you have thought of if there are too many risks to the children. If going somewhere vast, such as the seaside, delineate the boundaries within which the children are allowed to roam.
- Always be sure of having sufficient adults to look after the children safely. Make sure they are aware of their responsibilities.
- Children should hold hands when crossing a road or walking along a busy street. They should be constantly informed of the dangers of wandering off and the adults need to be constantly alert, counting the children and checking that no one has been left behind.
- Children need to be informed of what to do if they should get lost and have knowledge of a pre-determined meeting place, which should be written down.
- Lunch packs should not include any drinks in glass bottles, as these can break and become a hazard.
- Ideally, at least one of the adults should have a first aid certificate. Children needing medication on occasion, such as those with asthma, should be carefully supervised and the medication carried by an adult.
- All children should be transported wearing seat belts. When exiting from any form of transport children should alight on to the pavement, not the road.
- Children should never be left unsupervised when eating or playing near water.
- Children should be warned never to touch or eat anything found growing.

Partnership with parents

- Outings are a great opportunity for the establishment to share experiences with parents and children.
- Parents need concise and clear information about any proposed outing, so that they can give informed consent in writing.
- All parents should be welcome to attend outings, but care must be taken not to exert pressure on those parents who either do not want to or cannot come.
- If parents volunteer to take responsibility for children other than their own, they must understand the rules of safety and the aims of the curriculum, whilst acknowledging that the staff of the establishment have the ultimate responsibility.

Activity

Plan an outing for a group of five year olds, which will give them an insight into a culture other than their own. Write a letter to the parents giving them the information they require.

Resources

Godfrey S., 1992, *Environmental Activities*, Bright Ideas for Early Years Series, Scholastic Publications Ltd.

Heald G., 1996, *Journeys*, Themes for Early Years Series, Scholastic Publications Ltd.

Wade W. and Hughes C., 1994, *Inspiration for Environmental Education*, Scholastic Publications Ltd.

Dorling Kindersley, Eyewitness Explorers Series: *Birds*, *Seashore*, *Shells*, *Trees*, etc.

Lacey M., 2007, *First Nature Book*, Usborne.

Organisations

Community Transport Association, Highbank, Halton Street, Hyde, Cheshire SK14 2NY. Telephone: 0845 130 6195.

Visit London. Telephone: 0871 222 3118.

The Wildlife Trusts, The Kiln, Waterside, Mather Road, Newark, Nottinghamshire NG24 1WT. Telephone: 01636 677711.

NASUWT leaflet, Educational visits, Rose Hill, Rednal, Birmingham B45 8RS.

Websites

www.naturegrid.org.uk

www.uk-gallerydirectory.co.uk

www.visitlondon.com

www.wildlifetrusts.org

www.nasuwt.org.uk

15 Displays and Interest Tables

Displays can be on the walls, on tables, on display screens, on low chests and cupboards, done by adults, done by children or be a joint effort. It is usually quite easy to see which ones are which, and one needs to have clear aims for the displays.

Displays can be a mixture of children's two-dimensional and three-dimensional work, objects, resource books, posters, materials and reproductions of famous pictures, or they can focus on just one of the above. They should be educational and child-centred, not merely decorative. They need to observed, discussed and changed frequently. Children need the opportunity to examine and touch the displays. They should therefore always be accessible and at the children's level.

Displays and interest tables that revolve around a theme help children understand their environment and are particularly useful if they relate to an outing, which is in itself part of the curriculum. For example, a visit to the park where leaves, pieces of wood, feathers, nuts, conkers and other natural items are collected and displayed, help children to remember the outing, to examine the material more closely, to discuss with adults what they have observed and direct them to resource books to look up names and discover more.

Children should be involved in choosing, mounting and displaying the work. Being involved will make the display more relevant to the children, and the educational value will be increased.

 Activity

What is being displayed in your placement at the moment?

- Is the subject matter relevant to the children?
- Could the display be improved in any way? If so, how?
- What would be the best way to display some work that you have done with the children?

Essential materials

- Wall space at a suitable level and table tops
- Suitable mounting materials and tools for wall displays, and some material for covering the tables.

Practical tips for wall displays

If time permits, pictures look better if they are mounted. Choose a colour that complements or contrasts with the work. Light mounts make the work look darker and dark mounts make the work look lighter, so you need to try out different shades before reaching a decision.

The colour of the display boards can be changed by using backing paper.

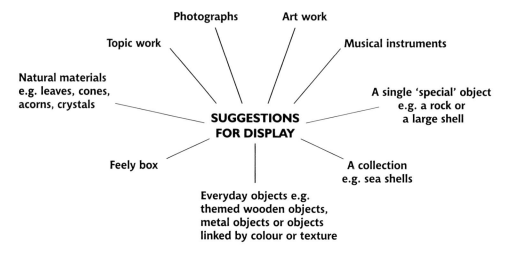

If labelling is required, the writing should be done in lower case, with a capital letter at the beginning. The writing should be clear and well formed. The following chart may help you with this task.

Links to the EYFS

Personal, social and emotional development

Displays encourage interaction between children and adults and shows them how to respect and care for others' work, to share ideas, to cooperate and to follow safety rules. Displays foster a sense of achievement and self-esteem. Some displays help children with their feelings, for example jealousy of a new baby.

Communication, language and literacy

Displays encourage discussion and stimulate listening skills. If labelling is used, the children may be able to 'read' the words.

Problem solving, reasoning and numeracy

Displays encourage mathematical skills, such as measurement, spatial awareness, patterns and shapes. They encourage children to think, ask questions, solve problems and make decisions. They stimulate memory recall.

Knowledge and understanding of the world

Displays help children to become aware of their environment and are pleasing to the eye. They help to make the room a happy and comfortable place. Displays can be linked to spiritual awareness, through a sense of awe and wonder.

Physical development

Children need all their gross physical skills, stretching, reaching, balancing and bending, as well as fine skills in gluing, cutting and placing when helping adults display their work.

Creative development

Displays offer children the opportunity to explore and handle different materials and textures, and should be a visual delight. Displays can be designed to stimulate a particular sense, such as smell or taste.

✓ Good practice: role of the adult

- All children's creative work should be treated with respect and nothing should be displayed without asking the child's permission.
- All work is valuable and all children should have their work displayed at some time or other, not just the most artistically talented.
- Displays are mainly for helping the children's learning and need changing as soon as the children start to ignore them.
- Children should be allowed and encouraged to handle objects on an interest table, and the adults should be available to discuss any questions or comments they may have. Good displays will stimulate and inspire discussion.
- The most successful displays and interest tables are those in which the children have participated the most.
- Children's paintings and drawings should never be cut just to suit the display, but torn paper will need trimming.
- When the display is ready to put up, kneel on the floor so that you can see how it will look from the child's level.
- The room should always be bright, clean and colourful, so never leave up torn and tatty displays.

Essential points

Anti-discriminatory practice

- Make sure that all the children have the opportunity to display their work or to contribute items. The work of all the children needs to be seen to be valued.
- Displays offer an opportunity to look at our multicultural diversity and for all the children and their parents to take part.
- Some displays could be tactile, such as feely boxes, whilst others could have very bright strong colours so that visually impaired children can participate.

Safety

- It is important that all children participate in displaying work, but obviously very sharp scissors, Stanley knives, glue and staple guns should be handled only by adults and not left lying around. Staple guns should not be used in the hall, as the children might tread on a fallen staple when they are using the hall for movement or PE.
- Displays should not be hung from the ceiling, placed near fire exits, cover fire regulations or other safety signs, placed over light switches, near alarm sensors or have glitter on them that might fall into the eyes.
- Objects chosen for an interest table need to be safe when handled. For example, there should not be anything too small, which might be inserted into an ear or nose, or choke a small child. Glass objects might break and wooden ones splinter, heavy ones could be thrown or dropped on a toe. Sharp objects could cut and fragile ones might break.
- If displaying food, it should be fresh and changed regularly.
- Paper is a fire hazard and some walls might not be suitable for display.

Partnership with parents

- **Displays are a visual way of sharing information with parents. They can be involved in the curriculum and enjoy seeing some of their children's work on the walls.**
- **The parents' notice board should be attractive and eye-catching. Old notices should be taken down when out of date or tatty.**

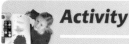

Activity

Set up an interest table for the children.

- Did it stimulate discussion?
- Did it convey information to parents and visitors?
- What did you learn from this display?

Resources

Andrew M., 2000, *Language Displays*, Scholastic Publications Ltd.
Beasley G. and Moberley A., 2000, *Seasonal Displays*, Scholastic Publications Ltd.
Dempsey S., 2001, *Story and Rhyme Displays*, Scholastic Publications Ltd.
Farrow V., 2000, *Our World Displays*, Scholastic Publications Ltd.
Finlay T. and Finlay J., 2000, *Maths Displays*, Scholastic Publications Ltd.
Harrison P., 2003, *An Eye for Display*, Belair Publications.

Websites

www.geocities.com/mydisplays

16 Festivals

There are a great many religious and cultural festivals to celebrate, from all over the world, and quite a few have become a part of all our lives, particularly those of our young children.

Religious and cultural festivals

Autumn term	Spring term	Summer term
Harvest Festival	Rastafarian Christmas	May Day
Rosh Hashana (Jewish New Year)	Chinese New Year	Dragon Boat Festival
Yom Kippur (Day of Atonement)	Shrove Tuesday	Carnival
Sukkot (Jewish Harvest Festival)	Ash Wednesday	Ra'·sha Bandhan (Festival of Sisters)
Ethiopian New Year (Rastafarian)	Mothering Sunday	Father's Day
All Souls' Day	Passover	American Independence Day
Divali (Festival of Light)	Ramadan*	Wesak
Guy Fawkes	St Patrick's Day	Pentecost
Remembrance Sunday	St David's Day	Whitsuntide
Thanksgiving	St George's Day	Festival of Hungry Ghosts (Chinese)
St Andrew's Day	Lent	Birthday of Haile Selassie
Birthday of Guru Nanak Dev Ji (Sikh)	Easter	Birthday of Muhammad
Hanukkah, also known as Chanukah (Jewish Festival of Light)	Eid-ul Fitr*	Janamashtami
Advent	Saraswati Puja	Shavuot
Christmas	Holi (Festival of Colour)	World Environment Day
Kwanzaa	Baisakhi	Raksha Bandhan
	Martin Luther King Day	
	Lantern Festival (Chinese)	
	April Fool's Day	

* Dates vary from year to year

It is important, because of our diverse multiracial society, to know about festivals celebrated by all the ethnic and religious groups in the UK, as well as the dominant Christian ones of Christmas and Easter and events such as Guy Fawkes celebrations. Because of this added richness, all our children will grow up with knowledge and respect for all cultures.

It is vital for children from all groups to feel that their culture and religion is respected and acknowledged by their peers. Groups of children from just one culture should also have the opportunity to explore other cultures and understand that we live in a multicultural society, far richer than they might have realised. Sometimes parents are not involved in advising and organising festival celebrations, and this can lead to misinformation and may even upset some parents.

Primary schools and nurseries use festivals as themes from which children learn. The example shown on page 135 uses Divali, the Festival of Light, as its central theme.

A Mehndi hand pattern

Essential equipment

It is not worthwhile celebrating any festival without having either a good supply of or access to relevant information, clothes, music, food, artefacts and books.

PES
- Celebrate the festival together
- Cook a rangoli together, learn to share and cooperate
- Hear the story of the victory of good over evil
- Discuss making new beginnings

MD
- Make shapes and patterns
- Sequence of the Divali story
- Discuss time – past, present and tomorrow

CLL
- Make a 'take home' book for the children to discuss with parents
- Learn songs and rhymes
- Tell the story and discuss it
- Write in Gujarati and Bengali
- Listen to tapes in several languages
- Make and write in Divali cards with small rangoli patterns

DIVALI

PD
- Listen and dance to Indian music
- Play appropriate instruments
- Smell and taste the food
- Dress up in appropriate clothes (sari day)

CD
- Make big rangoli patterns for display
- Block print patterns
- Portray the story in 3D
- Make divas from plasticine or clay
- Make mehndi patterns on hands
- Make candles and shadow puppets
- Make paper chains and hanging garlands

KUW
- Observe changes that occur in cooking
- Observe light and dark, and light and shadow
- Observe the effect of oxygen in burning
- Make a light house
- Computer images
- Relevant utensils and equipment in role play corner
- Possible visit to a temple

Links to the EYFS

Personal, social and emotional development

Festivals are a large social event, with the whole group working and planning together. Learning about cultures and religions other than one's own teaches respect. Understanding and asking questions about the moral codes of religions helps children to understand and develop their own ethical code. Celebrating festivals gives all the children a feeling of identity and self-esteem. It sometimes releases tension in its exuberance.

Communication, language and literacy

Learning new songs and poems aids children's vocabulary. Festivals offer an introduction to new language and an opportunity for group discussion. There are some well-illustrated books about festivals in many languages.

Problem solving, reasoning and numeracy

Food is often a part of celebrating festivals, and distributing it in the group may offer experience of one-to-one correspondence. Sometimes the food is cooked in the establishment, in which case there will be many opportunities for mathematical development, as there is in all cooking activities.

Knowledge and understanding of the world

Celebrating festivals can be spiritually uplifting. Children have the opportunity to create objects, use new textures and explore new materials. All areas of the curriculum can be explored and children can work at their own level or in a group.

Physical development

Festivals encourage children to dance and to play instruments, thereby using large muscles and fine manipulative skills in the making of masks, clothes, art and craft work and cooking.

Creative development

A festival is a feast for the senses: the smell and taste of different foods; the light and dark of Divali; the new musical experiences; and the rich tapestry of materials.

Activities

1. Describe the meals and cooking experiences provided in your placement.

   ● Do they represent the home cooking of the multicultural mix of the children?

   ● Are the children introduced to food from many cultures?

2. Look at the books and other resources in your placement.

   ● What variety of cultures and religions are represented?

   ● Is there anything you could bring in to add to the resources?

Good practice: role of the adult

● Celebrating festivals can dominate the curriculum if so many are chosen that little time is left for any other part of the curriculum. Plan carefully in advance, and make sure you are clear about the educational purpose and the relevance of the celebration.

● Remember that some families may not wish their children to take part in festivals, either due to their own religion or to their very strong anti-religious beliefs. Before embarking on a festival celebration, check with the families first and find out those who do not wish to participate, and those who wish to become involved. If you do have children who are not going to take part, make sure that you have an appropriate alternative activity for them and respect their parents' wish for their children not to be involved.

● Consult closely with parents or leaders of religious communities to make sure that you have the correct information. Not all members of an ethnic or religious group will celebrate in the same way and you must ensure that you do not offend or distress anyone.

● Any clothes or artefacts lent by parents must be handled carefully, but parents must be made aware that accidents can happen.

● If you have one or two children to represent the culture or religion you are celebrating, be careful not to keep on singling them out as you may embarrass them.

● Hallowe'en is not a suitable festival for very young children. There is no point in frightening children with horrific tales of witches and evil doings.

Essential points

Anti-discriminatory practice

- There is a risk of stereotyping if you celebrate festivals too extravagantly, and concentrate on the exotic side of their beliefs or culture. Respecting other cultures and religions should be an everyday occurrence, not a once a year wonder.

Safety

- Any festivals that celebrate light with open candles, such as Divali and Hanukkah, need very careful supervision.
- Most Guy Fawkes celebrations are very well monitored these days, although one still hears of death and injury. In the school or nursery situation, it is unwise to have fireworks and Guy Fawkes should only be remembered in verse, story and craft work. A discussion group could be held with teachers, parents and children warning of the dangers of fireworks, of walking the streets asking for money for the guy and of trick-or-treating at Hallowe'en.

Partnership with parents

- Festivals offer a good opportunity for the establishment to ask the advice and help of parents and to invite them to take part in the celebration.
- Be careful not to over-burden willing parents with too many demands for food or artefacts.

Resources

Addis I. and Spooner S., 1994, *Assemblies*, Scholastic Publications Ltd.

Everington J. and Jackson R., 1996, *KS2 Bridges and Religions*, Warwick Religions and Education Research Unit.

Court C., 2006, *Festivals*, Scholastic Publications Ltd.

Court C., 2000, *Multicultural Activities*, Scholastic Publications Ltd.

Evans J., 2004, *Festival Displays*, Scholastic Publications Ltd.

Fitzjohn S., Weston M. and Large J., 1993, *Festivals Together*, Hawthorn Press.

Fitzsimmons J. and Whiteford R., 1993, *Festivals and Celebrations*, Bright Ideas for Early Years Series, Scholastic Publications Ltd.

Godfrey S., 1990, *Christmas Activities*, Bright Ideas for Early Years Series, Scholastic Publications Ltd.

Kenyon P., 1999, *Festivals*, Scholastic Publications Ltd.

Palmer M. (Ed.), 2002, *The Times World Religions*, Flame Tree Publishing.

Rosen M., 1990, *Autumn, Winter, Spring, and Summer*, Seasonal Festivals Series, Wayland Publishers Ltd.

Sharp E., *Working Party on World Religions in Education*, National Society for Religious Education (Church House, Great Smith Street, London SW1P 3AZ. Telephone: 020 7898 1518).

Toys

For dolls and dressing-up clothes: see references to J. and M. Toys, page 70.

Websites

www.bradford.gov.uk/life_in_the_community/religion

www.ltscotland.org.uk

17 Information and Communication Technology (ICT)

By the end of the Foundation Stage, most children should be familiar with technology in their everyday lives and be able to use computers and programmed toys. The Foundation Curriculum encourages staff to introduce children to a wide range of ICT resources to support their learning.

These would include:

- computers and all related equipment including internet access
- programmable toys, including floor robots and remote control toys
- televisions, video recorders and cameras, radios, tape recorders, CD and DVD players
- telephones
- cookers, microwaves, fridges and toasters
- toy cash registers, swipe cards and other play equipment that reflects ICT equipment.

In this chapter we are focusing on the use of the computer at the Foundation Stage.

Nearly every child is excited and motivated by using the computer and is keen to explore new activities. Many children are familiar with computers from home and are keen to share this knowledge with other children in the group. Computers facilitate cooperation and discussion, and make for effective teaching and learning. You will find computers integrated into many existing play activities. For example, if a computer is used when playing 'shop', the customer can have a printout of the product, together with the price.

Computers can be used to enhance most areas of the curriculum, printing out appropriate cards and banners for festivals and birthdays, and using art software to illustrate their writing. Digital cameras can photograph food that is cooked in the establishment and the recipe can be put on the computer.

Computers have been known to crash and printers to jam, and it is important to have a knowledgeable person at hand so that staff and children do not become frustrated.

Amount of space		Type of space		Type of play		Adult involvement	
Whole area		Outside		Solitary	✔	Essential	
Half area		Inside	✔	Parallel	✔	Enriching	✔
Quarter area		Hard surface		Small group		Not always necessary	✔
Small area	✔	Carpeted		Large group		Can be intrusive	
		Table space	✔				

Essential equipment

- Computer with monitor, mouse and keyboard
- Built-in software
- Instruction manual
- Table and chair of a comfortable height.

Suggested additional equipment

- Printer and paper
- Memory sticks/CDs for storage
- External hard drive for back-up storage
- Appropriate CD-ROMs for the age group (e.g. 'PB Bear' series of interactive stories)
- Mouse pad
- Multimedia speaker system
- Digital camera
- Scanner
- Microphone
- Joystick
- Modem and access to the internet
- Lower case keyboard
- Computer trolley
- Tracker ball
- A paint programme.

Links to the EYFS

Personal, social and emotional development

Using the computer is sometimes a solitary occupation, but frequently children work together, although generally only one at a time can use the mouse. This encourages taking turns, sharing ideas and problem solving together. Support has to be frequently sought and given. Rules have to be understood and obeyed. Some games on the computer are competitive, and children have to learn how to lose gracefully and not gloat when they win. Self-esteem and confidence are gained with the successful completion of a programme. Using the computer can, and should, be an enjoyable activity. Patience and perseverance are learnt when problems occur.

Communication, language and literacy

Listening skills are developed, as understanding instructions is a vital part of computer expertise. Vocabulary is extended, as the language of computers has to be learnt. Exploration and experimentation are encouraged. Some games demand auditory discrimination and most require visual discrimination.

Problem solving, reasoning and numeracy

Using a computer aids concentration and problem solving. It can be used as a tool for gaining numeracy skills. Many programmes help children to understand the concepts of space, shape and measurement.

Knowledge and understanding of the world

Young children find it comparatively simple to understand modern technology and this helps with their knowledge and understanding of the world. There is easy access to images of the natural world. Following the rules for using any technology makes them aware of the need for safety in other areas. Using computers helps children to understand cause and effect.

Physical development

Fine manipulative skills and hand–eye coordination are promoted when using the mouse or the keyboard.

Creative development

Using a computer is a tactile experience. When pictures are created, they can be visually pleasing. Children can experiment with the paintbox, creating patterns and pictures, using sprays, brushes and pencils. There are CD-ROMs for young artists that encourage creativity and colour experimentation. They can work in two and three dimensions.

Activity

Start to construct a resource book of websites you have found useful, describing the content of each one. You might use the following headings:

- Site address
- Content
- Age group
- Child friendly?
- Comments

✔ Good practice: role of the adult

- Give all children opportunities to observe, discuss and use the computer regularly.
- Encourage children to work cooperatively and to share their skills and knowledge and become confident enough to try new activities.
- Make sure that no food, drink, sand or water is allowed near the computer.
- Ensure the children understand the rules of behaviour before allowing them to use the computer.
- Make the computer area look attractive, perhaps by displaying posters and information.
- Keep a record of which children have had time on the computer and what programmes they have used.
- Observe children regularly and keep a checklist of acquired skills.
- Always use the correct computer terminology.
- The ink in the printer should be checked regularly, particularly if the children are printing out pictures in colour. Make sure there is sufficient paper and spare ink cartridges in stock.
- Have patience and take time to explain the computing process.
- Ask for help if you cannot sort out a problem quickly.
- Cover the computer and printer at the end of each session and keep all equipment and disks away from bright sunlight.
- Show children how to handle CD-ROMs and disks correctly.
- Take advantage of any training, as technology changes all the time.

Activity

Send for some software catalogues featuring CD-ROMs suitable for young children.

- What might you select to support the six areas of learning and development?
- What games do you think have little to commend them? Why?

Essential points

Anti-discriminatory practice

- Some children will have frequent access to computers in the home and you may need to give priority to those children who have had little or no experience before attending the nursery or school. Encouragement may be needed for some children.
- A great deal of equipment is available for children with special educational needs, including concept keyboards and overlays.
- It is possible to slow the speed of the mouse for some children.
- The font size can be enlarged for those with visual impairment.
- Research has shown that even in these enlightened times boys are encouraged to use computers more than girls. You need to be aware that there might be this imbalance and to redress it if necessary.
- All software should show positive images of all cultures and both genders, and needs to be scrutinised for possible bias.
- Computers operated by various parts of the body can present learning opportunities for children with physical disabilities allowing access to the wider world. Programmes which teach in small steps can be helpful to children with learning difficulties.

Safety

- All equipment should be checked regularly and be well maintained.
- The computer table should be stable so that the equipment cannot be knocked or pushed over.
- The volume of noise should be regulated, so as not to harm hearing.
- All equipment needs to have appropriate plugs professionally fitted and there should be access to a number of power points.
- Computer cables should be stored out of the way of children.
- The monitor should be at an angle that makes children look up slightly when they are using it.

▶

- The chairs should have backs and be high enough for the children to keep their lower arms straight. Good posture is important to prevent injury.
- Wrists should be supported on the table or keyboard shelf.
- Never allow the children to play with the back of the equipment, linking cables or plugs.
- Ensure that every piece of equipment is switched off at the end of the day.
- Internet access needs to be closely supervised.
- Ensure that air can circulate around the computer.

Partnership with parents

- Many families have their own computer and will appreciate seeing their children becoming computer literate. Parents with expertise could help and support other parents and staff.
- CD-ROMs and other programmes can be shared and discussed.
- A workshop session may be offered to parents who are less familiar with computers.

Resources

Doherty G., 1998, *101 Things to do with Your Computer*, Usborne.
Farr A., 2001, *ICT Activities*, Scholastic Publications Ltd.
James F. and Kerr A., 1997, *Creative Computing*, Belair Publications.
Polly J.A., 2000, *Internet – Kids and Family*, Millennium edition, Osborne/McGraw Hill.
Wheeler T. and Short R., 1997, *101 Amazing Things to do with Your Computer*, Kingfisher.
Worrall P. and Mathieson K., 2003, *Art Through IT*, Belair Publications.

Websites
www.datec.org.uk
www.under5s.co.uk
www.dltk-kids.com
www.kudlian.net
www.mape.org.uk
www.teem.org.uk
www.becta.org.uk
www.earlyexcellence.com
www.letsfindout.com
http://education.staffordshire.gov.uk/Curriculum/Subjectareas/ICT

Part 4

Activities for the Infant School Child

All the activities that have been described in Part 3 are suitable for infant school children, although some will be extended further.

In Years 1 and 2 the children follow the National Curriculum at Key Stage 1 and this directs most of the children's learning activities.

Many children of this age attend breakfast clubs, after school and holiday clubs where they will engage in a wide range of play activities.

18 School and Out of School

Because delivering the National Curriculum takes up most of the school day, and is so tightly structured, there is not much space for students to show initiative in planning activities. Most teachers develop their long-term curriculum plans well in advance, and the students will assist in carrying them out. Whereas in the Foundation Stage the children will have a say in choosing their own activities, in the infant school the much tighter structure does not permit much latitude.

Learning through play

Although all schools vary, a good school will understand the importance of children learning through play, and through exploration. Hopefully, the children will not be told that they can 'play' when they have finished their 'work', but if this is so it is up to you to make sure the time allocated is used well, and the children enjoy and learn from their experience. Most schools will have set times for outside play, and it might be possible to make this more rewarding for them, by joining in their play and extending it.

Children of this age will go on more outings than the younger age groups. Outings provide a valuable learning experience and you will help the children make the most of them by listening to and answering their questions, finding books and resources to enrich visits, and extending the learning later in creative art, music or drama.

The National Curriculum

The English National Curriculum (National Curriculum) sets out the minimum curriculum requirements for all maintained schools, including:

- the subjects taught
- the knowledge, skills and understanding required in each subject
- attainment targets in each subject
- how children's progress is asserted and reported.

Within the framework of the National Curriculum, schools are free to plan and organise teaching and learning themselves. Many schools choose to use Schemes of Works from the Qualifications and Curriculum Authority. These help to translate the National Curriculum's objectives into teaching and learning activities for children.

Key stages

The National Curriculum is divided into four **key stages** that children pass through as they move up through the school system. These stages are in addition to the Early Years Foundation Stage described earlier:

- Year 1 and Year 2 of primary school are known as Key Stage 1
- Years 3 to 6 of primary school are known as Key Stage 2
- Years 7 to 9 of secondary school are known as Key Stage 3
- Years 10 to 11 of secondary school are known as Key Stage 4.

Subjects at Key Stage 1 and 2

The compulsory National Curriculum subjects for Key Stages 1 and 2 are:

- English
- Mathematics
- Science
- Design and technology
- Information and communication technology (ICT)
- History
- Geography
- Art and design
- Music
- Physical education.

Schools also have to teach:

- Religious education.

Parents have the right to withdraw children from the religious education curriculum if they choose.

Schools are advised to teach:

- personal, social and health education (PSHE)
- citizenship
- one or more modern foreign language.

There are **attainment targets** and a **programme of study** for each subject. Programmes of study describe the subject knowledge, skills and understanding pupils are expected to develop during each key stage. It's acceptable for schools to use different names for the subjects, as long as they're covering the National Curriculum.

The core subjects

English

Literacy sessions take place each day. The English programme of study focuses on:

- speaking and listening
- reading
- writing.

Activities children take part in include:

- drama activities
- reading stories
- recognising words from common spelling patterns
- using capital letters, full stops and question marks.

Mathematics

Mathematics is part of everyone's life. Children need to learn how to estimate, measure, solve problems and handle money. In the infant school, children explore mathematics through practical activities and discussion. They learn spatial relationships, quantities and how to solve problems. Much emphasis is placed on mental maths where children develop the ability to add, subtract, divide and multiply in their heads. A numeracy session will be held each day. The mathematics programme of study focuses on:

- number
- shape, space and measure
- handling data (in Key Stage 2).

Levels and formal teacher assessments

Attainment targets are split into **levels**.

Teachers carry out regular checks on children's progress in each subject. There will also be **formal teacher assessment** at the end of Key Stages 1–3. (Pupils will usually take GCSE/equivalent exams at the end of Key Stage 4). This indicates which National Curriculum level best describes individual children's performance in each subject. Schools send parents a report telling them what National Curriculum levels their child has reached in formal assessments.

For more information about the National Curriculum, follow the links at www.direct.gov.uk. For more information about the new secondary curriculum, visit the Qualifications and Curriculum Authority website at www.qca.org.uk.

Activity

An activity you might like to carry out in your infant school placement is a Piaget **conservation** test. These are ways of testing mathematical concepts in young children and quite often have interesting results.

According to Piaget, children of five or six years of age cannot conserve. This means that their thought processes are dominated by the appearances of things, and they do not realise that the volume of an object may not change just because the appearance changes. Conservation occurs when children are able to take in several features of the objects they are looking at all at the same time.

▶

You must be careful to be neutral and objective when administering these tests and be sure to praise the child whatever the answer.

Conservation of number

Show a child two rows of buttons, and ask him or her to count each row. When he or she has agreed that there is the same number in both rows, spread one row of buttons out. Then ask if either of the two rows contains more buttons. A child who cannot conserve will say that the spread out row must have more buttons.

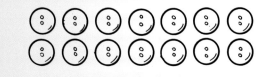

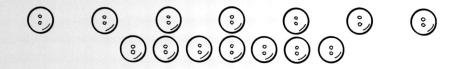

Conservation of mass

Show the child two balls of clay and get his or her agreement that both balls contain the same amount of clay. Then roll one of the balls into a sausage shape and ask the child if they still contain the same amount of clay. A child who cannot conserve will say that the sausage shape must contain more than the other ball, as it looks as if it contains more.

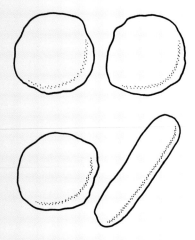

Conservation of volume

Ask the child to pour water into two identical tall thin jars until the child is satisfied that both contain an equal amount. Then, in front of the child, pour the water from one of the jars into a shorter but wider jug. A child who cannot conserve will say the tall jar contains more liquid.

Science

Science is all around us. Many daily activities are scientific: gardening, cooking and eating are just three examples. Science involves children in exploration, making predictions and comparisons, and testing out theories. All children ask questions about the world in which they live.

Science is divided into:

- scientific enquiry
- life processes and living things
- materials and their properties
- physical processes.

In the infant school, children will learn about plants, different types of sounds, sorting objects according to their properties, such as floating and sinking, and different textures. They will also explore what happens when heat or cold is applied.

✓ Good practice: role of the adult

- Make sure there is plenty of time and opportunity to explore and observe.
- There should be stimulating objects in the classroom to excite the curiosity of the children.
- Provide additional resources for further investigation.

- Make sure that all tools and equipment are kept in good order and that children know how to use them safely.
- Always employ the correct scientific terms when discussing experiments with the children.
- Ask open-ended questions.
- Show that you are curious yourself, and eager to discover and explore.
- Help children to record their findings by using photography, writing, drawing and computer technology.
- Consolidate the children's knowledge by constructing displays that will remind them of their experiments and explorations.
- Make sure the scientific resources in the book corner are up-to-date.

Non-core subjects

ICT

Although not a core subject, ICT is used throughout the curriculum as it makes teaching and learning more effective. It empowers children and is an ever-increasing significant factor in the outside world. Children are able to access the internet for information and research, and test theories.

✓ Good practice: role of the adult

- Talk with the children frequently, listen to them carefully and encourage them to ask questions. Respond as fully as you can and do not be afraid to look up anything of which you are not sure.
- Encourage them to concentrate on activities so as to extend the children's concentration span.
- Encourage them to share and join in activities with other children, so as to promote cooperation in the class.
- Tell them stories, and read and talk about books with them whenever possible.
- Encourage the children to look at books by themselves.
- Share songs and number rhymes, and look for an opportunity to teach new songs.
- Provide plenty of well-sharpened pencils and crayons, and give them time and opportunity to incorporate writing into their play.
- Introduce and explain as much new vocabulary as possible, particularly mathematical and scientific terms.
- Encourage counting and the use of numbers in all situations. Make children aware of the shapes in everyday objects.
- Spell words correctly and write clearly yourself.
- Praise children for their efforts, and show them that you appreciate all their achievements.

Activities

- Using clay with the children, ask them what they might like to make. The ideas should come from them. When finished, allow the clay to harden. The children may then paint what they have made and, after varnishing, the finished articles should last for some while.

- Read a book without pictures to the children. Ask the children to draw some scenes from their imagination, and make these drawings into a book.

- Buy some grass seed with the children. Choose different media on which to grow the grass, such as sand, earth, cotton wool, blotting paper and cardboard. Ask the children to measure and record which grass grows the fastest and which looks the healthiest? Why?

- Take a small group of children shopping with you. (You may have to take another member of staff as well, because, as a student, you are not insured to take children out on your own.) Having decided what they want to cook, let them buy the correct amount of ingredients, pay for them and make sure they have the right change. They will be able to weigh and measure everything themselves. Your role will be supervision and encouragement.

- Make a board game with the children that will help them with some aspect of mathematics. Your supervisor will tell you in what area the children in the class might need some extra help.

  (a) Write an observation of the children using the game.

  (b) Evaluate how well it works for the age group.

Playwork

Playwork provision for children outside school hours is found in many different settings such as:

- breakfast clubs
- after school clubs
- adventure playgrounds
- holiday play schemes
- play centres
- hospitals
- holiday clubs.

Many of these schemes are used by working parents. The activities provided are often difficult for parents to make available at home, such as woodwork or football, and so the provision is also used by parents who do not work, in order to give their children wider opportunities.

There is no pressure on the playworkers to follow a curriculum. Their role is to provide a safe, secure but challenging environment and to make available appropriate resources for play. Playworkers planning activities may have to take into account a wide age range, often from five years to 12 years, and sometimes up to 16 years.

Playwork principles

These principles establish the professional and ethical framework for playwork and as such must be regarded as a whole. They describe what is unique about play and playwork, and provide the playwork perspective for working with children and young people.

They are based on the recognition that children and young people's capacity for positive development will be enhanced if given access to the broadest range of environments and play opportunities.

1. All children and young people need to play. The impulse to play is innate (built in). Play is a biological, psychological and social necessity, and is fundamental to the healthy development and well-being of individuals and communities.

2. Play is a process that is freely chosen, personally directed and intrinsically motivated. That is, children and young people determine and control the content and intent of their play, by following their own instincts, ideas and interests, in their own way for their own reasons.

3. The prime focus and essence of playwork is to support and facilitate the play process and this should inform the development of play policy, strategy, training and education.

4. For playworkers, the play process takes precedence and playworkers act as advocates for play when engaging with adult led agendas.

5. The role of the playworker is to support all children and young people in the creation of a space in which they can play.

6. The playworker's response to children and young people playing is based on a sound up-to-date knowledge of the play process, and reflective practice.

7. Playworkers recognise their own impact on the play space and also the impact of children and young people's play on the playworker.

8. Playworkers choose an intervention style that enables children and young people to extend their play. All playworker intervention must balance risk with the developmental benefit and well-being of children.

The activities provided for children by playworkers will depend to some extent on the restrictions of the environment and the function of the setting. For example, a breakfast club may only provide table-top activities and books, and perhaps the opportunity to use the outside playground. At an adventure playground it would not be easy to find a place for quiet or solitary activities. Hospital play might be restricted to bed play. Some holiday play schemes might concentrate on one or more sports, particularly those at leisure centres.

Activity

Plan three activities for seven year olds on a wet day. One activity should extend creative development, one emotional development and one physical development.

Paul Bonel and Jennie Lindon in their book *Playwork: a guide to good practice*, suggest the playworker should be familiar with the following range of activities:

- choices in physical games and the chance to use physical skills, such as climbing and building
- some choices in craft and creative activities
- helping out in the routine of the play setting
- shared activities such as board games or cards
- time for conversation with other users and with the playworkers
- enjoyment of books and story time
- selected use of television or video
- the scope for imaginative play
- plenty of opportunities for free play and the encouragement to do this
- trips out, either local or more special trips further afield
- activities chosen to help children. For instance, playworkers in hospital have sets of play equipment specifically collected to help children come to terms with injections or the after-care stage of a serious operation.

Essential points

Anti-discriminatory practice

- All children should have access to all the activities.
- The children should be allowed some choice in the activities provided.
- Children with special and individual needs should be identified so that these needs are recognised and incorporated into the planning of the programme.

Safety

- Safety policies need to be written down and made available to parents.
- Procedures should be in place to ensure that children are not collected by anyone unknown to the establishment.
- The establishment should be aware of any medical conditions or allergies, and these should be recorded and made known to all staff.
- All equipment should be maintained and checked regularly and only used for its proper purpose. The outside sandpit should be covered when not in use.
- Suitable footwear and clothing should be worn by children and staff.
- All emergency procedures should be practised regularly.

Partnership with parents

- Time should be spent with parents explaining the ethos of the establishment.
- Clear and accurate information should be shared with parents.
- An effort should be made to make parents welcome.
- Encourage parents to take part in the sessions. Many parents will have talents, information, skills and resources that will be valued by the establishment.
- Reassure parents that children using the internet will not have access to undesirable sites, as firewalls or a barrier system has been installed.

Resources

Barnes R., 2002, *Teaching Art to Young Children,4–9*, RoutledgeFalmer.
Bonel P. and Lindon J., 2009, *Playwork: a guide to good practice*, Nelson Thornes Ltd.
Broadhead P., 2003, *Early Years Play and Learning*, RoutledgeFalmer.
Brown F. and Taylor C., 2008, *Foundations of Playwork*, Open University Press.
Davy A., 2000, *Playwork – play and care of children 5–15*, Thompson Learning.
Evans J., 2003, *Science: Early Years activities*, Belair Publications.
Hopkins C. et al, 2009, *Mathematics in the Primary School*, David Fulton.
Hughes B., 2002, *A Playworkers Taxonomy of Play Types*, Playlink.
Mosley J. and Thorp G., 2002, *All Year Round: exciting ideas for peaceful playtimes*, LDA.
National Playing Fields Association, PLAYLINK and children's Play Council, 2000, *Best Play – what play provision should do for children*, National Playing Fields Association.
Phinn G., 2000, *Young Readers and Their Books*, David Fulton.
Porter A. and Swift F., 2001, *Science Activities*, Scholastic Publications Ltd.
Rees J., 2002, *Fizz Buzz – 101 Spoken Numeracy Games*, LDA.
Uppal S., 2000, *Pocket Guides to the Primary Curriculum: ICT*, Scholastic Publications Ltd.
Williams D., 2003, *Step by Step Display in the Primary School*, Topical Resources.
Williams D., 1998, *Step by Step Art for Key Stage 1 Classes*, Topical Resources.

Websites
www.standards.dfes.gov.uk/beaconschools
www.show.me.uk
www.minedu.govt.nz
www.ipl.org/div/kidspace/
www.atschool.co.uk
www.londonplay.org.uk
www.naturegrid.org.uk

Part 5

Course Work

The satisfactory completion of practical work with children is required by various childcare courses of all levels, many having different regulations and requirements. This applies to college-based courses and National Vocational Qualifications. We have included guidance on how to evaluate your work, as this is an intrinsic part of becoming a professional childcare practitioner.

19 Course Work

Most childcare courses require you to plan, prepare, carry out and evaluate activities for the children in your placement. You may be on a course where you will have to plan your activities in detail and are required to submit a number of curriculum plans, detailed activity plans and routines, put together in a portfolio. For some Level 2 courses, you may be asked to undertake a number of planned activities that will be included in your portfolio.

As course requirements may change from year to year, we have not attempted to outline all the regulations. These will be found in your handbook, and your tutors will give you the necessary information, help and support in understanding the structure of the course.

By reading this chapter, we hope that you can begin to understand what will be required of you in placement and we have included some examples for you to consider.

Curriculum plans

'Curriculum' is the term used to describe all the learning, experiences, activities and opportunities that take place in any setting. A curriculum plan describes the range of activities or experiences offered to children to promote specific areas of learning and development, leading to appropriate outcomes according to the age of the child. See pages 165–9 for an example of a curriculum plan written by a Level 3 student.

The reason you are asked to write curriculum plans is so that you can plan activities confidently, recognising where and how learning occurs while incorporating anti-discriminatory practice and responding to the total development and learning needs of the child. You will learn how to plan, carry out and evaluate activities, and how to keep records that can be shared with the team and the parents. As you recognise and understand your contribution to the learning process, you will become more secure in your professional role.

Many settings break their planning down into three stages:

- long-term planning, creating a framework to give structure and coherence to the curriculum, usually for a year

- medium-term planning, addressing particular aspects of the curriculum in more detail, covering a term or half term
- short-term planning, considering children's individual needs and interests on a day-to-day basis.

When you devise a curriculum plan you will need to be clear about the aim and rationale of the plan, and the anticipated learning outcomes for both the child and yourself. You will be expected to describe briefly a number of activities related to the plan, each outlining a different learning objective within the plan.

Detailed activity plans

From each curriculum plan, you will be expected to describe two detailed activity plans, where you have carried out the activities with the children. See pages 166–8 for examples of detailed activity plans.

When you have completed your activity, you should ask yourself the following questions.

1. Did you succeed in carrying out your plan?
2. Did it differ in any way and, if so, why?
3. How did the children react?
4. Were there any health or safety issues?
5. Did all the children have equal access?
6. Were the resources adequate?
7. Was the activity stimulating enough?
8. Was the activity too complicated?
9. Did you have enough time to carry out the activity?
10. Did you have sufficient space?
11. Did you adequately protect the area you used?
12. Did the children learn what you thought they would learn?
13. Did they learn anything in addition?
14. Did you learn what you thought you would learn?
15. Did you learn anything else?
16. If you repeated this activity, is there anything you might do differently?
17. Did you manage to involve the children in the planning?
18. Did they willingly help you clear up after the activity?

Resources

You may be asked to produce resources that you have made yourself for some of the detailed activity plans. These might include:

- toys
- games
- musical instruments
- books
- audio tapes
- story props
- sensory materials
- mathematical or science packs
- displays or interest tables.

Your tutors will assess your resources for age-appropriateness, relevance to the activity and learning outcomes, anti-discriminatory practice, safety, durability and presentation.

Curriculum Plan 1, to provide activities for children of 3–4 years 11 months in the EYFS

Overall plan

Problem Solving, Reasoning and Numeracy

- Count in threes
- Make porridge (measuring)
- Sizes (big/medium/small)
- Wall display

Communication, Language and Literacy

- Sentence making
- Talk about the story
- Adapt/make up bear stories
- Read the book

Knowledge and Understanding of the World

- Of animals
- How are chairs made/materials
- Tell the story in different languages
- Link it to the real world

Chosen area for activities

GOLDILOCKS AND THE THREE BEARS

Creative Development

- Make collage pictures
- Drawing and painting
- Role play
- Make up songs/poems

Personal, Social and Emotional Development

- Share experiences (seeing bears/walks in the woods)
- How do the characters feel?
- Where they live
- Talk about morals (don't take other people's things)

Physical Development

- Act out the story
- Visit bears in a zoo
- Music and movement tapes
- Make houses, trees, chairs

Description of activities in chosen area

Activity 3
Talk about the story
What should Goldilocks have done/do? What did she do wrong? What is the same/different in the stories?

Activity 2
Sentence making
Get the children to write sentences they remember from the story – writing from left to right.

COMMUNICATION, LANGUAGE AND LITERACY

Activity 4
Read the book
Read different versions of the book, get the children to join in with parts they know.

Activity 1
Adapt/make up bear stories
Get the children to help a lost baby bear find his way out of the woods – drawing on worksheet.

Aim

To plan, organise and implement two activities, which help the children to develop and learn, within the Communication, Language and Literacy area of the Foundation Stage, under the theme of 'Goldilocks and the Three Bears'. In Communication, Language and Literacy children will read and write some familiar words and learn to use a pencil.

Activity 1

This should develop the children's fine manipulative skills and their ability to control and hold a pencil. It will also encourage the development of their social and observational skills and cognitive development.

Activity 2

This should develop the children's awareness and understanding of word and writing. This will be done throughout the Foundation Stage, in which children will develop pre-reading skills, which involve 'an awareness of print' and 'understanding that text is made up of words' (Tassoni & Hucker, page 118). It will also develop their memory and communication skills, by encouraging the children to talk about the pictures.

Rationale

The activities should help and improve the children's writing ability, develop personal, social and emotional skills and enhance language and communication.

These activities should help support the planning of the class teacher, by providing a different learning opportunity. These activities will provide the basic knowledge and first hand experiences for the children to be able to write, which will be useful in all other areas of the curriculum and away from the school setting. This agrees with Vygotsky's theories on cognitive development. He believed that children are active in their learning and that they develop an understanding through first hand experiences.

Activity 1

This underlines the children's ability to hold and control a pencil (fine manipulative skills) and therefore write; this agrees with Tassoni & Hucker 'Writing letters . . . requires quite skilled hand-eye co-ordination' (page 129). It encourages the child's concentration skills. I hope this activity will help the children to develop their descriptive skills and their ability to speak to and listen.

Activity 2

This will help the children to understand writing, that letters together mean something, starting points for writing and write left to right. They will develop memory skills and develop respect for each other, regardless of ability. They will also learn to express themselves by making comparisons/differences to the pictures. It will also develop the children's language and descriptive skills.

Learning outcomes for the children

Activity 1

I want the children to learn:
- Observational skills
- How to hold a pencil
- Listening skills
- Concentration skills
- Repetition – 'practice makes perfect'

Activity 2

I want the children to learn:
- Respect for others
- To be patient
- Listening and communication skills
- To make comparisons
- Memory skills
- To write left to right

Learning outcomes for the candidate

For both activities, I will learn to take the children's age and stage of development into account, as well as their writing ability. I will learn to use language that gets the children's attention and keeps their interest. This agrees with Bruner's theory; he believed that 'Adults maintain children's interests and point out information or give support that will allow them to increase their knowledge and reasoning' (Tassoni & Beith, page 132). I will learn to be aware of and to assess and adapt to the individual needs and requirements of the children. 'Observe progression on an individual level and use this to plan the next step' (Beaver et al, page 406). I will ensure full participation of the group including the slower and quieter children and that the activity is of value to them and that they will gain from it.

Evaluation

Activity 1

I chose to do this activity with a mixed group of children, so that I could pay more attention to their individual needs. At the beginning of the activity, I showed the children the worksheet and asked if they could help Baby Bear out of the woods, because he is lost. I gave the children a choice of colours they could use to help Baby Bear. I explained to the children that they needed to follow the path and that sometimes the path went around the trees . . . could they follow it? The children were very good at following the path – this showed me they listened to and understood the instructions. Occasionally the children missed some of the loops around the trees – this is possibly due to under-developed observational skills, and will improve with practice. The children were able to draw their lines close to the original path – this shows me that they were able to hold their pencils correctly. At the end of the activity, one of the children asked to colour in his worksheet – this shows that they enjoyed the activity and were not distracted by other things happening in the classroom. As a result I gave all the children this opportunity – all the children chose to colour in their worksheet – thus developing further their manipulative skills.

Activity 2

At the beginning of the activity the whole class was reading the book 'Goldilocks and the Three Bears'. When my small mixed group of children moved to the table, I reread a section of a different version of the story, about the chairs. As I read the story I pointed at the words occasionally starting from the middle of the line and sometimes reading the line backwards. Each time I did this I was met with laughter and shouts of 'NO!' from the whole group – this shows me that all the children were alert and listening/watching my actions. It also showed me that they understood the basics of reading. I then gave each child a worksheet with three different size chairs, with yellow writing. I asked the children individually whose chair was in the picture and explained that they need to start at the dots, when going over the writing; I also showed them which way to write (L-R) and how to hold the pencils correctly, to give them more control. The children completed the task well – showing me they had listened to the story, could remember it and understood the instructions. On one occasion, one child started on the dot, but completed the fourth line instead of the second. This would require practice to develop. I then finished off the activity by again asking the children whose chair was in the picture – this repetition will improve their memory skills and they were able to develop their reading skills by using their sentences to help them.

Evaluation of learning

For both activities, I think the children and I learnt all the things I previously stated in the proposed learning outcomes. I also learnt to ask questions, such as: Have you been to the woods? Did you get lost? How big is your chair at home? and I learnt to encourage comments from the children e.g. 'My house looks like that!' and 'There are lots of trees!', as this develops conversation and therefore language skills. I also learnt that the children like to colour in their worksheet afterwards – thus developing fine manipulative skills. I learnt a lot about the planning, timing and space that was needed for both activities. Without it I think the activity would not have been as successful, as the children would not have been kept interested and the activities could have been at the wrong stage of development for their age. As a result of being well organised, I was able to 'keep going', leaving less time for disruption in either activity. I also learnt that the children learnt differently when doing the activity with me rather than with the teacher. This may be as a result of different approaches towards learning between us. This agrees with Tassoni & Beith, 2nd edition, who say that 'Children benefit from the input of more than one adult; this . . . means that children benefit from different teaching styles' (page 306).

Recommendations

Activity 1

Occasionally the children missed some of the loops around the trees – this is possibly due to under-developed observational skills, and will improve with practice. I would encourage the children not only to follow the path, but to draw on it – as this would develop hand–eye co-ordination skills and pencil control 'As children become used to holding pencils and crayons, their hand movements will become more accurate and relaxed' (Tassoni & Hucker, page 29). I would also provide similar activities to do regularly that would improve the observational skills of the children. This activity would need to be repeated many times throughout the day either during literacy lessons, free time or at home.

Activity 2

On one occasion, one child started on the dot but completed the fourth line instead of the second. This would require practice to develop. In the future I would get the children to match up the words to the pictures – developing phonics and recognition skills. I would also get the children to copy the words from another source – rather than over the top of the writing – as this would develop skills of observation and may encourage them more to write L-R, reading would also develop their ability to do this. 'The English language is read from left to right and where possible children need to get used to moving in their eyes in this way' (Tassoni & Hucker, page 122).

With more time for both activities, I would develop and encourage understanding of the activity (What? and Why?), and future implications (Why are they doing this activity?). This agrees with Beaver et al, who said that adults need to help children to organise the understanding of what has happened, that is to draw conclusions and to form concepts' (page 407).

Resource

A resource is something you make that can be used again.

The resource I made was a story page and a worksheet, for Activity 2 (although I also made one for Activity 1). I wrote out a section of the story using a large font – making it easier for the children (including visually impaired children) to read and follow while I read. I also made it attractive – to interest the children. In Activity 1 the worksheet has big clear pictures of chairs and a large space to write sentences in.

I found that the learning resource was very effective, especially the story page, which can be used to develop the child's reading skills. I found that the children were pleased to be able to colour in afterwards as it gave their worksheet a 'stamp' of individuality.

Bibliography
A Practical Guide to Activities for Young Children – Hobart & Frankel, 2nd ed., Nelson Thornes Ltd (1999)
Babies and Young Children – Beaver et al, Nelson Thornes Ltd (2000)
Diploma in Childcare and Education – Tassoni & Beith, Heinemann (2002)
Early Years Child Care & Education: Key Issues – O'Hagan & Smith, Baillière Tindall (2002)
Planning Play in the Early Years – Tassoni & Hucker, Heinemann (2000)
Understanding Child Development – Sara Meadows

Routines

A 'routine' is an activity that happens on a regular basis, either hourly, daily, weekly or even annually. You may be asked to demonstrate your knowledge of a 24-hour routine for a baby under a year and to describe the daily routine within a placement setting to which you have contributed. Recording a routine helps students reflect on and evaluate their practice. The following routine was devised by a Level 3 student:

Aim: The aim is to provide a 24-hour routine for an 8-month-old baby, which takes into account all areas of development, all baby needs and requirements, while considering individual needs.

Environment: The baby in this routine is eight months old. It is in a home setting. There is a main playroom where the baby spends part of each day. She has one elder brother who is three years old and attends nursery.

24-hour routine

Time	Event
6.00 a.m.	Baby wakes up. Breastfeed
6.30	Nappy change
7.00	Free play
8.00	Breakfast
8.30	Wash, nappy change, dressed
9.00	Sleep / quiet time
10.00	Play (singing and music)
10.45	Snack and drink
11.15	Nappy change
11.30	Soft play – toys
12.00 p.m.	Lunch
12.45	Outside play
1.30	Water play
2.15	Drink

2.30	Nappy change
2.45	Sleep
3.45	Sensory activities
4.15	Tea
5.00	Story time
6.00	Bath
6.45	Breastfeed
7.15	Bed
11.00	Breastfeed
11.30	Sleep
6.00 a.m.	Wake up

8 Months

Areas of development	Norms of development	Toys/activities	Role of the adult
Gross motor	• May stand while holding on to stable objects • Can sit unsupported for longer periods of time • Moves by rolling • Get into sitting position from stomach • Able to move towards object out of reach • May bounce when held in standing position	• Peekaboo • Stacking games	• Provide opportunities to develop large movements • Provide adequate space, praise, encouragement • Encourage confidence and balance by placing toys around sitting baby
Fine motor	• Visually alert to people and objects • Pincer grasp developing • May be able to pick up small objects	• Simple musical instruments	• Allow plenty of time for play
Cognitive/ language	• Babbles loudly • Imitates sounds • Begins to understand commonly used words • May begin to watch others with interest	• Rhymes	• Talk to baby about everyday things • Use everyday events to encourage language development
Emotional/ social	• More wary of strangers • Likes to finger feed • Try to use bottle/cup • May be upset when main carer leaves	• Finger play • Safety mirror	• Involve baby in meal times

Routine

There are 13 basic needs of a baby and these need to be considered when planning a routine. These are:

Physical needs
• Warmth and clothing
• Routine

Mental and emotional needs
• Security
• Affection

- Activity/fresh air
- Sleep and rest
- Health care
- Safety
- Hygiene
- Food

- Stimulation
- Social contacts
- Independence

A baby's day needs to include six main aspects:
- Regular change of nappies
- Stimulation
- Opportunities for fresh air
- Time for love and cuddles
- Sufficient extended periods of sleep
- Sufficient feeds for their current age and weight

Regular changes of nappies

It is important to regularly change nappies as this can help prevent nappy rash, sores and infections. One of the main causes of nappy rash is when a soiled or wet nappy is left on too long – this allows ammonia present in urine to irritate the skin. Babies' nappies should be changed on average every three to four hours at feeding times and if necessary at other times. Nappy changing can provide a 'pleasurable contact time and opportunity for meaningful interaction between the baby and carer' (*A Practical Guide to Working with Babies*, A. Dare, M. O'Donovan, Nelson Thornes Ltd, page 66). This can help the baby to feel secure and loved. Also nappy changing can allow the baby to kick and move their legs more freely. This will help promote the development of physical skills.

When changing nappies it is important to remember the following health and safety points:
- The area where the baby is changed needs to be cleaned thoroughly to prevent cross infection.
- All hands should be washed before and afterwards.
- Gloves need to be used when dealing with body fluids.
- The area where the baby is changed needs to be safe and secure as at eight months babies are beginning to become more mobile and may be able to move around by rolling.
- Babies should never be left unsupervised.

Stimulation

At eight months a baby may be responsive to adults she knows and may be babbling. As a result of this I have included a specific time for music and singing. This will help promote language development, allow the baby to become familiar with different types and will introduce movement and rhythm.

The baby is becoming more mobile and active and as a result of this I have included outdoor play which will help promote physical development. Outdoor play which is suitable for 8 months include:
- Activity centres/ mats
- Sensory objects
- Choosing appropriate toys. These could be placed just out of reach to encourage mobility.

According to *Your Baby's First Year* (A. Mackonochie) at eight months babies are able to sit for longer periods of time. As a result of this, one play activity which I would provide would be an activity centre, which would help the baby to explore and develop new and existing skills.

Toys provided on activity centre:

- Baby safe mirror. Babies enjoy looking at their own reflection and this can help develop a child's self identity
- Rattle – will help to promote different sounds, textures, colours
- Bells
- Different textured objects
- Music and lights area.

Learning outcomes:

- This activity will provide appropriate stimulation to cover all areas of development, particularly sensory and physical development.
- It will help the baby learn about what happens when objects are touched etc.
- It will help the baby learn about different shapes, textures, weights.
- The toys provided will all help promote physical development, particularly fine motor as a baby manipulates the toys.

Role of the adult

- It is necessary to supervise the baby whilst playing, both joining in with the baby's play and also providing opportunities for independent play. By allowing the baby to play on her own, independence will be promoted and confidence will be gained as the baby learns new skills while focusing on activities and manipulating the toys.
- Provide appropriate stimulation and encouragement appropriate to the age and stage of the baby. Adults should observe the baby playing to ensure that the toys are safe and appropriate to the baby's development.
- Adults should talk to the baby, providing praise and introducing new vocabulary. By providing praise a baby will learn which behaviours and sounds to repeat so that a positive response is given. This can be linked to Skinner's theory. Skinner believed that 'language is learned after we are born through a process of reinforcement' (*Babies and Young Children*, Beaver et al, page 149). The positive response which a child receives 'encourages the child to repeat the sound or word' (Beaver et al, page 150). Words which are not praised or encouraged are not reinforced and therefore the child learns not to repeat these. This is based on the theory of operant conditioning. Skinner believed that social interaction between the carer and baby will result in the baby imitating adult sounds and attempting to repeat these.

Throughout the day I have incorporated several different activities which will help the baby develop and learn new skills, e.g. during water play at 1.30 p.m. where the baby will be able to experiment with the water the baby will:
- develop their physical skills
- try out different materials.
There should be a variety of resources which are developmentally appropriate for a baby. These could be simple toys such as water shakers, beakers.

When planning a water activity it is important to remember the following:
- The area and resources must be safe.
- There should be constant supervision with appropriate adult: child ratios.
- If children are uncomfortable or appear distressed when playing with the water they should not be forced to participate.

It is important that the environment is safe, hygienic and stimulating. 'Lack of stimulation in children's early lives can affect their later overall development' (*Diploma Childcare and Education*, P. Tassoni, page 105). Adults play a large role in providing an appropriate environment.

Opportunities for fresh air

It is important for babies to have some fresh air every day. This acts as a learning environment for children as well as providing vitamin D. Most of vitamin D comes direct from the sunlight so it is important that children receive 'a moderate amount of sunlight, especially during the summer months, so that they build up a store of this vitamin' (*Healthy Diets for Infants and Young Children*, page 8). Because of the importance of fresh air and exercise I have included outdoor play, which will help promote physical development and also help children learn about their environment.

Time for affection/one-to-one

Babies need adequate quality time with their primary carer. This will help the baby to form attachments and as a result will begin to feel more secure. By eight months a baby should be securely attached to their primary caregiver and may display signs of separation anxiety when separated. Although this baby is in a home setting there will still be times where the baby is separated from the caregiver.

John Bowlby researched into the area of attachments and observed 'that there seemed to be a pattern to the way children reacted if they were separated from their main attachments' (*Diploma Childcare and Education*, P. Tassoni, page 259)

He concluded that there are three main stages of separation anxiety:

Stage	Signs
• Protest	• The child may cry but is easily comforted.
• Despair	• May appear withdrawn, no longer looks for attachment figure.
• Detachment	• When main figure returns he/she is ignored

It is important that the baby receives adequate affection to cater for their individual needs. This involves playing games, cuddling the baby, providing stimulating activities, talking to the baby. By providing the baby with affection the baby will learn to trust and respond to people and will begin to have more secure attachments.

Sufficient extended periods of sleep

'All babies are very different in their needs for sleep and rest and in the ways they can be settled'. Sleep and rest play a vital role in a baby's development:
- Without sleep, concentration, memory and mood are affected.
- When we sleep body functions slow down, allowing the body to rest and recover.
- Having enough sleep is particularly important to children because during sleep growth hormones are released from the pituitary gland.
- While children are sleeping it allows them to begin to make sense of and understand the day's events.

(*Diploma Childcare and Education*, P. Tassoni et al.)

As a result of the importance of sleep I have provided several times throughout the day where the baby will be able to sleep or rest. Adults should help encourage children to sleep but they should not be forced. If children do not wish to sleep they are still able to rest. To help encourage children to sleep:
- Adults could provide a quiet activity before sleeptime. This could be reading or singing. It will also provide close comfort to the baby, encouraging security and familiarity. The baby will begin to learn about routines.
- It may be necessary for a baby to be provided with a comfort object, such as a blanket or toy.

D. Winnicott focused his research in the 1960s and believed that:
- Play is essential to social and emotional development.
- He identified comfort objects which children become particularly attached to. They are often described as transitional objects as they help to remind a baby of their home environment and primary carer, where they feel secure. They can help lessen the effects of separation or help comfort a child who appears distressed. A comfort object 'can provide comfort and reduce anxiety' (*Applying Psychology to Early Child Development*, C. Flanagan, 1996, page 37).

Sufficient feeds for their current age and weight

At eight months a baby should be well into the weaning process. Weaning is where solid foods are gradually introduced into the baby's diet. Signs that a baby is ready to be weaned include:
- waking early for feeds
- not settling to sleep after feeding
- still being hungry after breastfeed
- may show an interest in other food.

Weaning is an important process for babies because milk doesn't provide all the nutrients a baby requires over the age of six months. Weaning can help babies become less dependent on milk and introduces new tastes and textures to a baby's diet. 'Babies at around six months are ready to learn to chew food. The muscular movement helps the development of the mouth and jaw and also the development of speech' (*Babies and Young Children*, M. Beaver, J. Brewster, Nelson Thornes Ltd, 2001, page 487).

Between seven and nine months the baby's nutritional requirements are 825 calories for boys and 765 for girls. As a result of this it is particularly important that the baby's diet is balanced and includes food from each of the four main food groups. These are:
- Milk and dairy foods → Growth and development, good vision
- Meat, fish and other alternatives → Iron, which helps body to carry oxygen, Zinc, which helps wounds to heal, Proteins, which are used for energy, growth and repair
- Bread, other cereals and potatoes → Carbohydrates, which provide energy. This is particularly important as children become more active and mobile as they develop
- Fruit and vegetables → Vitamins and Minerals.

At eight months old this is a suggested weaning plan:

On waking	Breastfeed
Breakfast	Mashed Weetabix, toast soldier, water
Snack	Pieces of ripe banana, water
Lunch	Puréed chicken, green beans, potatoes
	Yoghurt, water
Tea	Cheese sandwiches, Water
Evening	Breastfeed

According to *A Practical Guide to Working with Babies*, 2nd edition, A. Dare, M. O'Donovan, page 119, from seven months pieces of hard foods such as peeled apple or carrot can be given. As a result of this I have incorporated pieces of ripe banana which can also be given as finger foods.

Between eight and nine months a baby can begin to join in with family mealtimes. Mealtimes can help promote independence as a baby learns to use her own cup and spoon and can help social development. It should be remembered that every baby is an individual and that not all babies at eight months will be ready to hold a cup etc. Chewing promotes exercise for the jaw, which as a result can help language development. Children should only be introduced to a family mealtime once a baby is able to sit. It is important that the baby sits in a high-chair and that the harness is always worn. This prevents the baby from falling.

Babies need more iron on their diets as their own stores are lower after the age of about six months. Extra nutrients are needed as the baby becomes more active as they attempt to crawl and walk.

Routines

Routines play a vital role in a child's overall development:
- Having a familiar routine helps children to feel secure.
- Routines 'can help children to feel secure and settled, while still allowing them time to explore, play and learn' (*Planning Play and the Early Years*, P. Tassoni. page 52).
- Routines provide a structure to children's lives, which can help children learn to know what to expect and helps child to become familiar with daily activities.

When planning routines it is particularly important that the routine if flexible. This is so that the child's needs can be catered for. Every child has their own needs and as these needs change the routine may need to accommodate for this. Routines still need to be structured enough so that children become familiar with them.

It is important that the routine is linked to the age and stage of the child. This is so that the child's developmental and individual needs are met throughout the day. If the routine isn't developmentally appropriate then the child will not benefit from the play opportunities provided and will not help to promote overall development. The activities and experiences need to interest and stimulate the children in order to promote development.

Routines are also one aspect of care which can provide learning opportunities:
- Routines provide opportunities for the development of physical skills.
- 'Provides opportunities for social interaction, for example eye contact and smiling' (*Babies and Young Children*, Beaver et al, 2001, Nelson Thornes Ltd, page 32). By interacting with children this can help the child to feel loved, wanted and secure.

References and Bibliography

A. Dare, M. O'Donovan, *A Practical Guide to Working with Babies*, 2nd edition, Nelson Thornes Ltd, 2002, pages 65–67, 119–120.
A. Mackonochie, *Your Baby's First Year*, Anness Publishing, 2001.
M. Beaver, J. Brewster, *Babies and Young Children*, Nelson Thornes Ltd, 2001, pages 32–33, 149–150, 487.
P. Tassoni, K. Hucker, *Diploma Childcare and Education*, Heinemann, pages 105, 258–259.
C. Flanagan, *Applying Psychology to Early Child Development*, pages 35–37.
P. Tassoni, *Planning Play and the Early Years*, Heinemann, page 52.

Other Resources

Booklet: 'Healthy Diets for Infants and Young Children', page 8.

Portfolios

You may be required to compile a portfolio of your curriculum plans, detailed activity plans, resources and routines. It must include a table of contents and contain a statement declaring the authenticity of the work.

Level 2 courses may require you to keep a portfolio of all your work undertaken in the placement. It may include diaries, logs, observations, additional activities you have carried out with the children, and examples of leaflets and records from the placement. Your portfolio activities will be included, as well as references and a bibliography.

Your placement supervisor must sign all pieces of work. Confidentiality must be maintained at all times, and parental permission obtained in writing for any material that might identify the child or the family. It is your responsibility to make sure that your portfolio is kept in a safe place. Obtain a receipt if you hand it over to your tutor or supervisor.

You may, as an NVQ candidate, be asked to compile a portfolio of a range of activities that you have carried out with children.

To help you ensure that your assignments have covered all the essential areas you should think about the following points:

Practical considerations

- Discuss your proposed activity with your supervisor, assessor or line manager. Make sure your establishment has the resources and materials you need, considering the cost within the total budget.
- What safety and anti-discriminatory issues are relevant to this activity?
- Ensure that the activity is age-appropriate.
- Plan the timing: decide how long it will take and agree with other staff when you are going to carry out this activity.
- Remember to protect the area, if necessary, and the children's clothing.

Value of the activity to the children

- What areas of development will this activity extend and promote?
- How can the children be involved in the planning, setting up and clearing away of the activity?
- How does this activity link in with the EYFS?
- What opportunities are there to improve communication and build relationships?

Evaluating the activity

- Describe how it went with the children and with your supervisor, assessor or line manager.
- Had you planned it adequately?

- Did you feel the children were fully involved?
- Did you think it went well?
- How could you improve it next time?
- What were the benefits for the children and for the establishment?

Complete the evaluation forms on pages 180–4 of the Appendices.

The more activities you plan and prepare the more skilled and competent you will become. As you evaluate your planning and the implementation of your activities, you will become a professional and reflective practitioner.

Resources

Websites

http://education.staffordshire.gov.uk/Curriculum/Strategies/Early Years/
www.foundation-stage.info/resources

Glossary of Terms

Aesthetic/aesthetically – concerned with beauty or the appreciation of beauty.

Age-appropriate – activities that are suitable for the age and stage of development of the child or children.

Anti-discriminatory practice – working with children in a way that makes sure the individual needs of the children are recognised and met. Making sure that no child is discriminated against, and that all resources, language and behaviour in the establishment are appropriate.

Conservation – a mathematical term to describe the awareness that a number of objects that are equal in volume, length, weight or amount remain equal in spite of the appearance being changed. For example, two identical balls of clay remain the same even if one is re-shaped into a sausage shape.

Constructive criticism – critical appraisal of your work by your supervisor or line manager that helps you to improve your performance and that you are expected to accept.

Core subjects – those subjects that have to be taught.

Creativity – bringing into existence something original. It includes the ability to invent and research, and select a wide range of materials, tools and instruments. Creativity also includes imagination, feelings and ideas that lead to an understanding of art, music, drama, stories and imaginative play.

Curriculum – a course of study. The way that children learn, as well as what they learn, encompassing their whole experience and influencing all areas of development.

Development – the acquisition of new skills, ideas and attitudes that lead to progressive change.

Evaluation – the term used by childcare practitioners to assess and appraise observations and activities so as to plan for the future.

Growth – an increase in size that is measurable, generally to describe height, weight and head circumference.

Hand–eye coordination – the way that sight and hands are used together to complete a task, for example threading a needle.

Hypothesis – a proposal made as a starting point for further investigation into an area of research.

Implementation – carrying out a task.

Key worker – the person who has responsibility for the overall care of the child, writing observations, providing activities, keeping records and liaising with parents.

Malleable materials – pliable materials that respond to pressure, such as clay.

Milestones – significant events in the development of a young child, for example sitting up without help or learning to read.

Objectively/objectivity – making judgements from collected data and not allowing one's own feelings to be of any consequence.

One-to-one correspondence – a mathematical term describing how a child matches one number to each object.

Open-ended questions – questions that require more than the answer 'Yes' or 'No'.

Peer – a member of one's age group.

Positive images – developing an environment that reflects all the children in a positive way, avoiding stereotyping by race gender or disability. It should be reflected in books, posters, food, festivals and artefacts, and in the involvement of all the parents.

Recyclable materials – the current correct term for junk modelling materials.

Reflex – an involuntary reaction to stimuli, such as blinking.

Sensory – feeling through the senses: vision, hearing, taste, touch and smell.

Spatial relationship – learning to be aware and to control one's body in relation to space, other objects and people so that children can move safely and with confidence.

Stimulus – a situation or action that needs a response. For example, the smell and sight of dinner will make a hungry child run to the table, eager for her food.

Supervisor – a qualified person who will support the student in placement, assessing progress and writing reports.

Symbolise – using an object to represent something else. For example, using a brick and pretending it is a gun.

Tactile – the adjective that describes touch.

Vocalisation – sounds made by a baby before expressive speech.

Appendices

Activities for children in the infant school

Language in the National Curriculum

Proposed Activity: _____

Describe how some of the concepts below may be developed or encouraged during the activity.

Listening:	Stories	
	Music	
	Conversation	
Talking:	Discussion	
	Conversation	
Writing:	Early pre-writing	
	Writing	
Reading:	Pre-reading	
	Handling books	
	Reading	

This page may be photocopied. © Nelson Thornes Ltd.

Activities for children in the infant school

Mathematics in the National Curriculum

Proposed Activity: _____

Describe how some of the concepts below may be developed or encouraged during the activity.

Conservation	
One-to-one correspondence	
Sequencing and counting	
Shapes	
Sorting	
Spatial relationships	
Time	
Symbols	
Patterns	
Money	
Estimating and measuring:	
Weight	
Height	
Width	
Volume	
Capacity	
Quantity	
Mathematical language	

This page may be photocopied. © Nelson Thornes Ltd.

Activities for children in the infant school

Science in the National Curriculum

Proposed Activity: _____

Describe how some of the concepts below may be developed or encouraged during the activity.

Exploring	
Using the five senses	
Gathering information	
Discovery	
Sorting and classifying	
Recording	
Experimenting	
Making changes	
Predicting and making hypotheses	
Scientific language	

This page may be photocopied. © Nelson Thornes Ltd.

All Activities

Evaluation of activities

Activity: _____

What went well?
What went wrong?
Did you meet all the aims of the activity?
Did the activity allow active collaboration and involvement of the children?
What would you change in future plans?
How would you follow up this activity?
How does it link to future activities?
For infant school activities: how did you involve the children in the learning process?

All Activities

Monitoring for anti-discrimination/anti-bias

Activity: _____

How does the activity encourage collaborative learning at some point in the process?

List the opportunities for the development of language.

How does the structure of the activity provide access for all the children?

How could the activity recognise the validity of all the children's cultures and backgrounds?

How does the activity encourage children to develop social and interpersonal skills?

This page may be photocopied. © Nelson Thornes Ltd.

General Resources

Books

Brown B., 1998, *Unlearning Discrimination in the Early Years*, Trentham Books.

Bruce T., 2001, *Learning Through Play – Babies, Toddlers and the Foundation Years*, Hodder & Stoughton.

Casey T., 2005, *Inclusive Play*, Paul Chapman.

Dabell J., 2009, *Classroom Gems: Games, Ideas and Activities for Primary Mathematics*, Longman.

Department for children, schools and families, 2008, *Early Years Foundation Stage – Everything you need to know*.

Drake J., 2003, *Organising Play in the Early Years*, David Fulton.

Einon D., 1998, *Dorothy Einon's Learning Early*, Facts on File Inc.

Hall N. and Abbot L. (Eds), 1994, *Play in the Primary Curriculum*, Hodder & Stoughton.

Herr J., 2001, *Creative Learning Activities for Young Children*, Delmar/Thompson Learning.

Hobart C., Frankel J., and Walker M. (Series Editor), 2009, *A Practical Guide to Working with Parents*, 2nd edition, Nelson Thornes.

A Practical Guide to Child Observation and Assessment, 4th edition, Nelson Thornes, 2009.

Good Practice in Safeguarding Children, 3rd edition, Nelson Thornes, 2009.

Hyder T. and Kenway P., 1995, *An Equal Future: a guide to anti-sexist practice in the Early Years*, National Early Years Network.

Jeffree D. and McConkey R., 1994, *Let Me Play*, 2nd edition, Souvenir Press Ltd.

Jordan, S., 2002, *Songs and Activies for Early Learners: Pre-School and Primary*, Jordan Music Productions.

Kaffner T., 1999, *The Pre-schoolers Busy Book: 365 creative games and activities to occupy your 3–6 year old*, Meadowbrook Press.

Lear R., 1990, *Play Helps*, 3rd edition; and 1993, *More Play Helps*, Heinemann.

Lindon J., 2001, *Understanding Children's Play*, Nelson Thornes Ltd.

Macintyre C. (Ed.), 2001, *Play for Children with Special Needs*, David Fulton.

Matusiak C., 1990, *Maths Activities, Bright Ideas for Early Years Series*, Scholastic Publications Ltd.

Morris J. and Mort L., 1990, *Learning Through Play and Getting Started, Bright Ideas for Early Years*, Scholastic Publications Ltd.

Mukherji P. and O'Dea T., 2000, *Understanding Children's Language and Literacy*, Nelson Thornes Ltd.

Newman S., 2008, *Small Steps Forward: Using Games and Activities to Help Your Pre-school Child with Special Needs*, Jessica Kingsley.

Rappaport Morris L. et al, 1989, *Creative Play Activities for Children with Disabilities*, 2nd edition, Human Kinetics.

Sangster M. and Catterall R., 2009, *Early Numeracy: Mathematics Activities for 3–5 Year Olds*, Continuum.

Sher B., 1998, *Self-esteem Games*, Jossey Bass.

Sheridan M. et al, 2007, *From Birth to Five Years: Children's Developmental Progress*, 3rd edition, Routledge.

Statutory Framework for the Early Years Foundation Stage, Department for Children, Schools and Families.

Tassoni P., 2008, *Penny Tassoni's Practical EYFS Handbook*, Heinemann Educational.

Uppal H., 2004, *Play Activities for the Early Years*, Brilliant Publications.

Whitebread D. (Ed) and Coltman P., 2008, *Teaching and Learning in the Early Years*, 3rd edition, Routledge.

Whitehead M., 2009, *Supporting Language and Literacy Development in the Early Years*, 2nd edition, OUP.

Wilkes A., 2003, *Activities for all Year Round*, Usborne Publishing.

Series

Blueprint Series is a series of practical ideas and photocopiable resources for use in primary schools, published by Nelson Thornes Ltd.

New Bright Ideas Series, Creative Early Years Series and Themes for Early Years Series are published by Scholastic Ltd, FREEPOST (SCE 2665), Windrush Park, Range Road, Witney, OXON, OX29 0YZ.

Practical Pre-school, Step Forward Publishing Limited, St Jude's Church, Dulwich Road, London, SE24 0PB. A magazine, books and resources for the Early Years Foundation Stage, including What Learning Looks Like Series:

Personal, Social and Emotional Development

Physical Development

Mathematics

Knowledge and Understanding of the World: Science and Technology

Language and Literacy

Communication, Language and Literacy

Helping Your Child with Mathematical Development.

Playmatters National Association of Toy & Leisure Libraries publish a range of practical resources that can be used with young children including their annual Good Toy Guide.

Websites

www.everythingpreschool.com

www.pre-school.org.uk

www.smallfolk.com

www.scholastic.co.uk

www.teacherstuff.org.uk

www.educate.co.uk

www.kididdles.com

www.teachingideas.co.uk

www.fuaim.ie

www.thebigbus.com

www.funwithspot.com

www.teachingideas.co.uk

www.gryphonhouse.com/activities

www.theideabox.com

www.sitesforteachers.com

www.natll.org.uk

www.practicalpreschool.com

www.standards.dcsf.gov.uk/eyfs/

www.everychildmatters.gov.uk

www.dcsf.gov.uk

www.direct.gov.uk.

www.qca.org.uk.

www.pre-school.org.uk

www.ndna.org.uk

www.ncma.org.uk

www.enchantedlearning.com

www.preschoolrainbow.org

www.preschoolexpress.com

Catalogues and equipment

Community Playthings, Robertsbridge, East Sussex TN32 5DR, Freephone: 0800 387 457, www.communityplaythings.co.uk. Also available free on request from Community Playthings is a full colour catalogue of special furniture and equipment for children with disabilities.

Galt Toys, Sovereign House, Stockport Road, Cheadle, Cheshire SK8 2EA. Telephone: 0161 4289111. Website: www.galt.co.uk

Hope Pre-School Catalogue, Hyde Buildings, Ashton Road, Hyde, Cheshire SK14 4SH. Telephone: 08451 20 20 55. Website: www.hope-education.co.uk

NES Arnold, Hyde Buildings, Ashton Road, Hyde, Cheshire SK14 4SH. Telephone: 0845 120 4525. Website: www.nesarnold.co.uk

Rompa, Goyt Side Road, Chesterfield, Derbyshire S40 2PH. Telephone: 0845 230 1177. Website: www.rompa.com (Products for children with sensory difficulties)

Teaching Trends, educational materials for teachers and parents, 160 High Street, East Finchley, London N2 9AS. Telephone: 0208 444 4473. Website: www.teachingtrends.co.uk

Organisations

BAECE, 136 Cavell Street, London E1 2JA. Telephone: 0207 539 5400. Website: www.early-education.org.uk

Dcsf Publications, Telephone: 0870 000 2288. Website: http://publications.dcsf.gov.uk

Disabled Living Foundation, 380/384 Harrow Road, London W9 2HU. Telephone: 0845 130 9177. Website: www.dlf.org.uk

National Children's Bureau, 8 Wakeley Street, London EC1V 7QE. Telephone: 020 7843 6000. Website: www.ncb.org.uk

National Early Years Network, 77 Holloway Road, London N7 81Z. Telephone: 0207 607 9573.

National Playbus Association, Brunswick Court, Brunswick Square, Bristol BS2 8PE. Telephone: 0117 916 6580. Website: www.playbus.org.uk

Play Board Northern Ireland, 59–65 York Street, Belfast BT15 1AA. Telephone: 028 9080 3380. Website: www.playboard.org

Play Scotland, Midlothian Innovation Centre, Pentlandfield, Roslin, Midlothian EH25 9RE. Telephone: 0131 440 9070. Website: www.playscotland.org/

Play Wales, 25 Windsor Place, Cardiff CF1 3BZ. Telephone: 01222 468 606.

Pre-School Learning Alliance, The Fitzpatrick Building, 188 York Way, London N7 9AD. Telephone: 020 7697 2500. Website: www.pre-school.org.uk

Save the Children, Centre for Young Children's Rights, 1 St John's Lane, London EC1M 4AR. Telephone: 020 7012 6400. Website: www.savethechildren.org.uk

Playmatters National Association of Toy & Leisure Libraries, 68 Churchway, London NW1 1LT.

World Organisation for Early Childhood Education (OMEP), 14 Bewick Court, The Holloway, Wolverhampton WW6 8NT. Website: www.omepuk.org.uk

Education departments

In London: Museum of Mankind, The Commonwealth Institute, Science Museum, Natural History Museum, Bethnal Green Museum of Childhood.

The Tate Galleries nationwide.

Safety organisations

British Standards Institute, 389 Chiswick High Road, London W4 4AL. Telephone: 020 8996 9001. Website: www.bsi-global.com

Lion mark: BSS 5665/EN71, the toy industry symbol for safety and quality, was introduced in 1989. For more details write to The British Toy and Hobby Association, 80 Camberwell Road, London SE5 0EG. Telephone: 0207 701 7271. Website: www.btha.co.uk

Royal Society for the Prevention of Accidents (RoSPA), Edgbaston Park, 353 Bristol Road, Birmingham B5 7ST. Telephone: 0121 248 2000. Website: www.rospa.com

Index

Page references in *italics* indicate illustrations and diagrams.